Nickname: The Smiling F

Educated: University of Sydney

Called to Bar: 1948

Took silk: 1974

Retired from the bar: 30 June 2000

Famous cases: Successfully defended Detective Sergeant Roger Rogerson on bribery charge and Judge John Foord, accused of attempting to pervert the course of justice. Counsel assisting the Royal Commission into the convictions of Lindy and Michael Chamberlain; counsel assisting the Blackburn Royal Commission; appeared for NSW Minster for the Environment Tim Moore in ICAC's inquiry into the Metherell affair in 1992.

Courtroom style: Dour but deadly.

Outside court: Shy and private family man who enjoys birdwatching and gardening. Married for over fifty years to Jean, a former science teacher. Three daughters. Five grandchildren.

By the same author

Walking on Water: A Life in the Law
Conviction of the Innocent

The Gentle ART OF PERSUASION

CHESTER PORTER QC

RANDOM HOUSE AUSTRALIA

Random House Australia Pty Ltd
Level 3, 100 Pacific Highway, North Sydney, NSW 2060
http://www.randomhouse.com.au

Sydney New York Toronto
London Auckland Johannesburg

First published by Random House Australia 2005
Paperback edition published 2008

National Library of Australia
Cataloguing-in-Publication Entry

Porter, Chester, 1926-.
The gentle art of persuasion: how to argue effectively.

ISBN 978 1 74166 795 0.

1. Public speaking. 2. Persuasion (Rhetoric). 3. Communication Skills.
I. Title.

808.51

Cover illustration: 'The Advocate' by Honore Daumier © The Corcoran Gallery of Art/Corbis
Cover design: Christabella Designs
Typeset in ACaslon 12/17pt by Midland Typesetters, Australia
Printed and bound by Griffin Press, South Australia

10 9 8 7 6 5 4 3 2 1

To my dear Jean

Contents

Introduction

The gentle art of persuasion

MUCH OF LIFE IS spent arguing, whether at home, at work, or in whatever situation we may find ourselves. Most arguments are futile, a waste of time. Neither the participants nor the audience learn anything. At their most extreme, arguments can even lead to physical fights. Yet intelligent argument is often the only sensible way to advance our many causes, to spread knowledge and to achieve progress.

One of the most successful early television shows presented Warren Mitchell as the hopelessly argumentative Alf Garnett in the BBC comedy 'Till Death Us Do Part'. It was a very funny illustration of the futility of unintelligent argument. Not only was Alf himself hopeless in trying to convey his ideas, but so were his family around him. They demonstrated that mere assertions were not proved facts, that arguments became, if anything, less convincing if shouted, and that nothing was achieved by losing one's temper. They were exaggerated characters, but their fame was achieved by their closeness to real life.

For an argument to serve a meaningful purpose, the participants, or at least one of them, must learn the art of persuasion, one of the more difficult skills to acquire in life, but yet one of the most useful.

Frequently, new ideas in business, commerce and even in science and medicine can only be effectively conveyed to others by persuasion. The art of persuasion – the ability to argue convincingly and effectively – is a skill that we all need to acquire.

Everyone needs to learn how to argue and how to persuade. Everyone who acquires these arts should employ them wisely and ethically.

I hope that this book will be of assistance to budding advocates, be they barristers or solicitors, but at the same time it is intended to reach a much wider audience. This book is intended to aid anyone who wants to argue convincingly whether he or she be a politician, parson, priest, barrister or solicitor, whether he or she be scientist, teacher, doctor, social worker, entrepreneur or union official.

The fundamental object of this book is to encourage honesty of thought, clarity of expression and the ability to persuade others. These are not easy objects to achieve.

Unfortunately, the art of persuasion is not easily acquired from books. Books and lectures can help a would-be persuader but experience is the only real teacher. To learn by experience is to learn the fool's way: by making mistakes – sometimes very serious mistakes. But it is hoped that readers of this book will acquire the art of persuasion more quickly and with fewer mistakes on the way.

Probably the most common mistake in this field is to try to be a good persuader by copying someone else who is acknowledged to be a good persuader. Thus a budding politician may seek to be a Winston Churchill or a John F. Kennedy and the result is usually disastrous. One must be oneself. One can improve on oneself, but one cannot successfully be a good persuader by trying to be someone else. An actor works on a pre-arranged script. A persuader has to work on his or her own script.

My own experience will perhaps illustrate some propositions about persuasion, which I will discuss in more detail throughout the book.

At school I was quite a good debater and captained my school's debating team against the teams of other schools. Team debating teaches valuable lessons in performing tasks and keeping to the point, and I acquired a good deal of experience in these.

Unfortunately, school team debating introduces people to advocacy too early. In advocacy, you put forward arguments in support of a proposition, regardless of whether you believe in it yourself. Team debating teaches you to do just that.

Although I gained a great deal of experience in debating at school and later at university, I soon learned that there were many negatives in team debating. Emotion tended to be feigned rather than real, and arguments were made in order to win debating points from adjudicators, rather than to convince the audience. Young speakers, and older ones too, tended to be smart show-offs and at times the distinction between wit and lack of manners became blurred.

I was a university adjudicator and I saw and heard many debaters, some of whom later became barristers. Team debating no doubt taught fluency, verbal skills and slick argument. But I think the real ability to persuade is a different skill altogether.

At university, I far preferred the parliamentary debates, the weekly Union Nights modelled on the Oxford Union where causes were debated by those who believed in them. My experience began there as a seventeen-year-old student among much better debaters.

When one has been a schoolboy captain of debating, there is a tendency to lose modesty as one is cheered by sympathetic audiences. My initial lack of success at

Sydney University soon revived much of the modesty I had lost at school.

Here I may deal with a speaker's problem that afflicted me and many others, but for which there is often a very simple solution. Ray Watson, later QC and still later Justice Watson of the Family Court, was a brilliant speaker at university, but not always a kind one. On one occasion he described the two previous speeches as 'rotten speeches, one bass and one soprano'. Mine was the latter and there was justification for the comment. I had difficulty with voice production. Ray's remark was par for the course in the University of Hard Knocks.

He then did me a favour later that night. He taught me a simple technique. You breathe in before you speak and let the words leave your mouth with the air so that you speak from your chest rather than your throat. It is so simple, and, with a little practice, works for most speakers, male or female, so that the voice volume increases enormously. As one learns to control one's voice, self-confidence increases.

From Union Night, I acquired valuable experience. I became a member of the Debates Committee, and then an inter-Varsity Debates Selector (for team debates). I also became an adjudicator, a judge of team debating. As an adjudicator, one learns a lot from watching for the achievements and mistakes of others.

However, I think the best public-speaking teacher I

had was the Rostrum Movement. I found Rostrum soon after I became a barrister in 1948. By that time I thought I was quite a good speaker from my school, university and post-university experience, but soon I found out that I was nowhere near as competent as I thought.

Rostrum Clubs are still running. In a Rostrum Club, one speaks to an audience that meets at lunchtime on a subject, according to one's actual beliefs. A speech need not necessarily be persuasive or try to be persuasive, although in my experience the majority probably were.

At the end of the meeting, an experienced speaker, called a Critic, or Speaker of the Last Word, would discuss and criticise the speeches. Some critics were very severe; others perhaps too gentle. If one could withstand and learn from tough criticism, one would learn quickly.

Back then, Rostrum (as I think it does now) contained a fair cross-section of the community, people bonded by a desire to be good speakers and by a general interest in the topics discussed. As the years went by, I appreciated that Rostrum members were very similar to an intelligent jury. They were a little more interested in what goes on in the community than the average person, but they held most of the ambitions, beliefs and prejudices of the general community.

Rostrum revealed to me many mistakes I, and most other people, made as a speaker, matters that I shall discuss in detail later in this book.

One of the fundamental matters I learned was the importance of attempting to understand your audience. For example, if one is trying to advance the cause of factory safety, the arguments that might persuade employees will differ from those likely to convince the employers. Even the arguments in favour of preserving bushland will vary, for example, as to dedicated 'Green' followers contrasted with timber workers. A good general will consider the likely opposition army and so will a good persuader.

I worked hard to improve myself in Rostrum, and eventually became a Rostrum critic, by election. I failed in my first attempt when I was very anxious to succeed. I thought it was not quite right to vote for myself and I lost by one vote. My successful opponent voted for himself. In future elections for various positions, I thought again about voting for myself.

As a critic, one learns a great deal. It is very hard and concentrated work, but, if done carefully and skilfully, one may detect not only the faults and mistakes but also the achievements of the speakers criticised. A good critic will detect the latter matters and give them as much prominence as the faults, so that the learners in the audience may find out what might succeed as well as what might fail.

Of course, as a critic or adjudicator one often feels, 'Physician heal thyself'. In Rostrum, critics subjected themselves to criticism by other critics. It was at times an unpleasant, if beneficial, experience. As a young barrister, I realised that even if the critic was wrong in his criticism of me, he was a juror whom I had failed to convince.

My experience in persuasion included some years in politics, about twenty from the age of twenty-one. I was an office-bearer and active member of the Liberal Party and became Bob Askin's campaign director in his own electorate, including the campaign that put him into power. (And before I joined the Liberal Party, I was vice-president of the first Liberal Club at Sydney University.) I heard many, many political speeches.

Political activity is often stimulating, but can also be very boring at times. Some political meetings are quite dreadful. However, one could learn a lot, particularly from presiding over meetings, as I often did. Chairmanship is an art in itself.

I was a member of the Liberal Party until the late 1960s when I was a member of Ted St John's campaign committee. He had left the Liberal Party, and I and many others supported him as an independent candidate for the seat of Warringah in Sydney. He lost. I was not formally expelled from the Party, but my membership was not renewed.

I have often thought since then that I gave up Hornby trains too early and politics too late, but the latter was a learning experience. However, I did achieve quite a lot in the Liberal Party.

I also had many years' experience as the president of a progress association and that involved many submissions to the local council. A progress association is made up of interested persons from a locality, intended mainly to make submissions to the local council. Most of the submissions oppose proposed developments in the area and progress associations can often be more correctly termed 'anti-progress associations'. Local politics are time consuming, but interesting.

I have been on numerous committees, a member of a church council, and an office-bearer in various associations. Through this experience, I have learned that committees, in particular, involve the art of persuasion.

I spent five years as an articled clerk, twenty-six further years as a junior counsel, and then twenty-six years as a Queen's Counsel. These were years of argument and, I would hope, persuasion.

It is with this background that I seek to pass on some of the many lessons which I learned, in the main, the fool's way, by experience.

Some people are very hard to convince and some causes are difficult indeed to advance to the wrong audience. For example, an argument for a republic is difficult to advance to the Coldstream Guards. However, the fundamental point is that if you understand how your audience is thinking, then you will choose your best arguments and advance them in ways least calculated to offend, and best calculated to convince.

This book is largely concerned with verbal argument, but much of it may be applied to written argument. I shall point out some of the significant differences in techniques.

I have already made the distinction of advocacy. An advocate argues for a cause with which he or she may or may not agree. An ordinary argument concerns what the persons actually believe. It is useful to note here that an advocate has an advantage over a mere arguer. The arguer is far more likely to lose his or her temper and that is the fundamental error of attempted persuasion. Alf Garnett, the idiotic arguer in 'Till Death Us Do Part', made all the usual mistakes, and lost his temper as a matter of course.

We all should be able to put our arguments intelligently and persuasively. There are many times in life when this ability is very necessary indeed.

At least twice in my life I had to persuade (successfully) a would-be suicide not to do it. I claim no training as a counsellor, but I followed the fundamental rules. I found out as much as I could as to what was causing the problem by encouraging the person to talk. Only when that person was petering out as to his or her complaints about life did I venture any counter-argument. By then I could realise what arguments were likely to be effective.

Such are extreme illustrations of the necessity to understand your audience, be it large or small, or only one person. They also demonstrate the need for patience.

If one has a fairly quick mind, patience is a virtue that is difficult to acquire. It is even more difficult if one is overworked, ill, tired or distracted by other matters. Yet impatience is one of the main reasons for failure as a persuader. Impatience can lead to rudeness, loss of temper, blundering and crass stupidity. If you doubt this, consider the drivers on the road and road rage.

One of the many keys necessary to open the padlocks preventing success as a persuader is that of restraint. A calm mind will think clearly; a considered reaction is much safer than a quick one. At the same time, a persuader often finds it necessary to think and act quickly. The ideal is to be patient, to listen, and, when necessary, to be quick to reply. It is not easy.

It is one thing to sound impressive, to devastate the opposition, to make a great impression. It is by no means the same thing to change people's minds, to convince them by your arguments. Persuasion is achieved, more often than not, by quiet rather than devastating argument.

There is one final thought in this introduction. The late Vic Hall, a fine member and one-time President of Rostrum, earned his living teaching advertising in what was then Sydney's only School of Advertising. Most of the past leaders in this difficult profession went through his school. Vic Hall taught me that ultimately it is impossible to maintain a successful advertising campaign for a poor product, whether it be a car, a machine, a medicine, a cosmetic or whatever. Ultimately the product will be tried and used and will have to prove itself. This is a simple application of the truism that ultimately the truth will out.

There is no substitute for quality and this applies to arguments, however well expressed. The argument that will ultimately prevail will be a valid one. Of course, this is only ultimately, but the object of a persuader should always be truth.

1.

The meaning of persuasion

WHEN THE FAMOUS BUSHRANGER Jack Doolan, on the last day of his life, met troopers Kelly, Davis and Fitzroy, he was, to say the least, outnumbered. When he was called upon to surrender, the ballad 'The Wild Colonial Boy' tells us:

> He took a pistol from his belt
> and waved it like a toy
> 'I'll fight but not surrender,'
> cried the wild colonial boy.

He left this world after his defiant speech, the memory of which is over a century old. This was an emphatic, defiant speech of confrontation. He did not seek to persuade the troopers to let him go.

The distinction between persuasion and confrontation is often not properly appreciated. As the president of a progress association, I took some pains in dealing with the council to avoid confrontation, and instead used gentle persuasion to try to achieve various objects for my district. I noticed, with some surprise, that my approach was not the usual one adopted by many other progress associations.

Progress associations tended to be 'protest associations' at perpetual war with the council. Accordingly, when they wrote to the council, the temptation to let off steam, and say in barely respectable terms what they thought of the council, was irresistible. Such letters no doubt made the writers feel good and may well have been preserved as historical items, but they were unlikely to effect desirable changes. Authorities confronted rarely yield to mere protest. They must be persuaded, and the task of persuasion is handicapped rather than assisted if the relevant authority is insulted in the process.

It is not unknown for young professional persons, new in practice with a freshly acquired letter-head, to write very belligerent and often downright insulting letters. It does feel good to let off steam, but the scalded recipients of belligerent or downright insulting letters do not like it, and start thinking in terms of payback. Such confrontational tactics are far from the gentle art of persuasion. Anything that provokes, enrages or even annoys the person or audience is going to retard, not advance, the prospect of persuasion.

It is important to put some stress on the word 'gentle'. The hard-sell approach once so popular with door-to-door salesmen, during which the customer never gets a word in edgeways, is an old-fashioned failed technique. In order to persuade, one should not provoke or insult or put offside the person or persons one is seeking to persuade. The fundamental approach in persuasion is to create a sympathetic mind in the person to be persuaded. By gentle persuasion, the person or audience is persuaded by reasonable arguments to adopt a different viewpoint, to change their mind. (The bludgeon or club approach has nothing to do with gentle persuasion.)

Parliamentary debates can be studied with these thoughts in mind. It is a parliamentary tradition that the opposition must be attacked, derided, belittled and insulted. Our democracy seems to assume this, although we are far less enthusiastic politically than other more volatile people. In the Liberal Party, I once heard a speech by a Serbian which ran:

'And so let us go forward. Let us destroy the Communist Party, the Labor Party, the Country Party and all the other traitors.'

In his mind politics should be played for keeps.

The parliamentarian hopes to belittle the opposition, rather than persuade it, but he or she also hopes to persuade the public that the cause advocated is worth adopting and the party advocating it should be supported. So parliamentary speeches tend to be both confronting (in relation to the opposing party) and persuasive (in relation to the general public – the electorate).

Party members love to cheer on speakers who 'dish it out' to the opposing party, and hence insult and accusation tend to prevail over persuasion. Solid argument tends to be lost in mere vituperation. The good parliamentarians try to rise above the standard slanging matches – the curse of democracy since the days of the Athenian state, which expelled its hero Themistocles and executed its greatest philosopher Socrates, as the result of wild speeches in the Assembly.

When a new bill is introduced into our parliaments, it is usually accompanied by a persuasive speech aimed at both the opposition and the electorate. Most bills pass unopposed, and often with enthusiastic support from all parties. When there is a dispute, then there tends to be the mixture of confrontation and persuasion that I have discussed. Parliaments are probably at their worst in question time when prime ministers, premiers and ministers seem to believe that the electorate will be most impressed by rudeness and insult to opposition questioners, rather than by facts and information.

In court cases, only a very foolish advocate will confront or insult the tribunal that is going to decide the case.

On the contrary, there is often an attempt to flatter the judge. However, the position is quite different if there is a jury, particularly in a criminal trial.

At times, judges interfere in trials directly, or with some subtlety, almost always in favour of the Crown. Appointment to the bench seems to make some appointees law-and-order addicts, loyal to the status quo and far above society's unfortunates, so that they assume that all accused persons are almost certainly guilty. Most judges are wise enough to keep such thoughts to themselves but some cannot restrain themselves and interfere in the trial. If counsel for the defence is succeeding in cross-examining a witness, the judge may interrupt and suggest that the successful questions were unfair. Counsel may be accused of improper conduct, or anything else to throw defence counsel off balance. On such occasions, confrontation of the bench by counsel, in front of the jury, is one possible course of action that may well succeed. Another tactic is to be scrupulously, even excessively, polite to a rude, interfering judge. The object in either situation is to persuade the jury by either loud confrontation or more subtle politeness that the accused is not getting 'a fair go' from the bench.

On one occasion, I adopted the latter tactic of politeness towards an interfering judge, and, when he came to sum up, the jury was so disgusted with him that they looked the other way while he was speaking. Of course, the accused was acquitted, despite a very strong Crown case.

The alternate approaches to the interfering judge illustrate the difference between confrontation of the judge, and gentle persuasion of the jury.

I tend to take an optimistic view of human nature, in general. I do not agree that people are biased with their minds forever made up in favour of prejudice.

Those who have had similar experience to me of criminal juries will usually agree that these juries are remarkably fair, impartial and open to reasonable persuasion. This is particularly so now that juries contain both sexes in approximately equal numbers.

When women were first eligible to serve on juries they had to apply, whereas the service of men was compulsory. We barristers then thought that the women who went to the trouble of applying were probably a bit unusual, and too risky to have on a jury. So these pioneer women were usually challenged and never served.

When jury service was made compulsory for both sexes, there could by and large be no challenge to their inclusion for reasons of gender. There were not enough challenges available, particularly when the number of challenges without cause (peremptory challenges) was drastically reduced. We barristers found ourselves with female jurors, whether we wanted it or not.

In my experience, it was a great reform. Women were

both conscientious and fair, but the real achievement of the reform was that juries now reflected the combined wisdom of the sexes. It has been shown that this combined wisdom is very useful in juries, company boards, committees, councils and even benches of judges. It might well be said that two sexes are better than one.

With modern juries, consisting of both sexes, and better educated, much of the old styles of emotional shouting (even weeping) which occurred in my early days at the bar (the 1940s and 1950s) ceased to be effective. The new juries wanted to be persuaded by logical, reasonable arguments. Their minds were open, even in very nasty cases involving serious offences. Whatever their prejudices, these people could be reached by careful argument. Their conclusions were usually correct on the evidence.

During periods of public hysteria, such as the paedophilia crusade, in my experience, and that of other counsel, juries have kept their heads and preserved the integrity of justice. They have put their prejudices aside and done their duty.

Of course, jury service is a solemn duty and it might be said that human nature generally cannot be judged by the conduct of jurors. I do not agree. Jury service simply serves to demonstrate that nearly everyone tries to do the right thing if you reach them. The same desire to do the right thing is apparent in all walks of life. People are constantly surprising with their kindness and generosity, as the Australian response to the Boxing Day 2004 tsunami disaster demonstrated.

So an important part of the art of persuasion is reaching the audience: finding the approach and the argument that will gain attention and convince. It is not easy, but persuasion is a worthwhile art, and far more attractive than noisy confrontation.

Yet there are some reasons, but there are other reasons that may be convincing arguments.

In the last Liberal Party meeting I ever attended, a small suburban branch meeting, there was an address by Robert Askin, then Premier of New South Wales. In the relevant part it was:

'Government has its difficulties. There are problems that arise and you will not all always like the way we solve them. Some problems are very difficult. Take the problem that confronted my friend Sir Henry Bolte recently in Victoria. Was this man Ryan to hang or not?

'Some people wanted him hanged and some wanted him reprieved. Sir Henry had to judge whether the majority of votes were for or against hanging him, and make his decision.'

Perhaps democracy can go too far.

I have distinguished between confrontation and persuasion. It is many years now since Dale Carnegie, a pioneer in public speaking and personal development training, made the important distinction between argument and persuasion in his bestselling book *How to Win Friends and Influence People*, first published in 1936. His book is not so frequently read today but many of his points are worth remembering. He advocated avoiding arguments in one-on-one conversations because if you won you provoked, if you lost you were humiliated. (Carnegie gives the word 'argue' a rather aggressive connotation, as, I suppose, is often the case in one-on-one disputes.) Rather should you avoid contradiction by saying the other person is wrong but let the other side talk itself out. Then you may apply gentle persuasion.

Carnegie advocated respect for the other person's opinions, and I would apply this to meetings as well as conversations. He was averse to telling people, at least directly, that they were wrong, but of course this may be unavoidable in a meeting or when persuading an audience. Still, one cannot be too tactful about telling people that they are wrong. Only an aggressive preacher such as Savonarola, the fanatical Dominican friar who sought to reform Renaissance Florence, can do this in a hostile way and get away with it – but did he? He was executed in the end.

Before I leave Carnegie's teachings, it is worth mentioning his advice to admit it quickly when you are wrong. It is surprising how many people choose to live with their errors rather than retreat. In my experience, it was a common fault of witnesses.

Carnegie's distinction between 'argue' and 'persuade' is important. I have not always preserved the distinction in this book, but it may be correct to say that argue tends to dispute, whereas persuasion may well be achieved without any dispute at all.

However, the word 'argument' is often used, particularly in courts, as meaning a stated reason for the desired persuasion. Nevertheless, the fact that persuasion can be achieved without a dispute is worth remembering, because this concept tends to stress the idea of not annoying or provoking the person or body of persons to be persuaded.

If possible, persuasion should be achieved gently. This is not always possible, as I shall discuss later in the book.

The ways to reduce confrontation are to hear the other side out, and in rebutting the opposing arguments do so in a way which will preserve the honour of those advancing those arguments. Respect should, if possible, be paid to the opposition. If an argument is open to easy demolition, do so gently. Next time it may be your argument.

2.

The ethics of persuasion

As I have already explained, at the end of a Rostrum meeting the critic makes the final speech consisting of a criticism of the chairperson and the speakers, aiming to point out the mistakes and achievements of the participants, so as to instruct them, and also the whole meeting. This method of instruction and improvement has proved very successful and many Rostrum members, myself included, learned a great deal from critics.

It was generally considered that great care had to be taken in criticising subject matter. A speaker was free to say what he or she wanted to, and the critic was not there to criticise the speaker's ideas and opinions, but only the manner of expressing them.

I was a critic for Rostrum for many years. Much more than most critics, I did deal with the subject matter of speeches on the basis that it was very difficult to make a good speech with poor subject matter or an inadequate topic. So I would criticise the lack of substance in a speech and the line of argument, but never the opinions of the speaker.

There was a particular meeting that strained my ability as a critic and the whole basis of Rostrum criticism. One of the speeches had been an overwhelming success and the speaker had sat down to sustained applause. When I rose to make the criticism, the audience expected only praise. They were disappointed.

It was not so long after the Second World War that many of us would not have heard or remembered the speeches of Adolf Hitler and Joseph Goebbels. Even as children many of us had lived through the war that those speeches had produced. This particular Rostrum speaker was using the same techniques, the raw appeal to the emotions, the perverted logic, the concocted lies, and I said so. It caused quite a stir and few critics ever dared to pursue the same line, but my message was understood. It was important that it should be understood.

I shall try to repeat the same message here. A good speaker, or, for that matter, a good writer, has a powerful weapon in his or her hands. A person possessing a talent for persuasion is a trustee of that talent for the good of the community. He or she should not abuse it.

The concept of ethics in persuasion is easy to state but difficult to apply. Of course, it does not mean that opinions contrary to one's own must be wrong and therefore should not be expressed, but it does mean that opinions should be honestly held and honestly expressed. It particularly means that the end does not justify the means.

Hitler's techniques were to lie and appeal to the raw emotions of the audience. (By raw emotion, I mean appealing to the primitive instincts of an audience, the classic example being the appeal for vengeance to a lynch mob, but there are much more contemporary examples; such as fear of Muslims or illegal immigrants or Aboriginal rioters, or even fear of losing one's precious property.) Hitler illustrated Dr Johnson's famous saying: 'Patriotism, sir, is the last resort of a scoundrel.' This clever half-truth was almost a prophecy of the Nazi nightmare.

It is important for members of a democracy to be able to recognise and expose the Hitler techniques of dishonest persuasion. I shall endeavour to state and illustrate some of them.

The first and most important is that a lie, apparently uttered with sincerity, if constantly repeated, ultimately will be believed. In Germany, between the First and Second World Wars, people were eager to find scapegoats for the sad and sorry condition of the country. Who better to be the scapegoats than Europe's perennial scapegoats, the Jews? Constant repetition of old, even medieval, lies turned them into proved truths. The Nazis created generally believed 'truths' by constant assertion of lies.

Although it is true that ultimately most lies will be exposed and the truth revealed, this may take many years or even centuries in the case of political lies. The truth about Europe's Jews was substantially revealed in the years after the war, but in the meantime there had been the Holocaust. The lies that made the gypsies also victims of the Holocaust have probably still not been unravelled, at least to the extent that gypsies are understood and not persecuted.

The recent book *In Hitler's Bunker* by Armin D. Lehmann, one of the Hitler Youth members who held off the Russians in the last days of Berlin in 1945, shows how the lies about the Jews became axioms of truth in the minds of Germans. Lehmann was indoctrinated as a boy and one can hardly blame him for what those around him taught him before he was old enough to be discerning about ideas. But many adult, well-educated Germans were persuaded to believe nonsense, by constant repetition of lies and censorship of the truth. Perhaps there is also an unattractive aspect of humanity that makes us too ready to believe scandal and evil.

The next Hitler technique is the false appeal to, and the perversion of, the better feelings of the audience. In the case of the Nazis the appeal was to patriotism. Now patriotism within reason, despite Dr Johnson's famous quote, is a fine thing, but the patriotism of the Nazis went beyond all reason, to the point of believing that Germany was the master race entitled to living space at the expense of the Slavs and anyone else whose lands were desired. Assertions of these propositions constantly repeated quickly turned them into fundamental beliefs.

How were the obvious logical flaws in the Nazi case concealed? This was done by appeals to the emotions. One such emotion was love of country – patriotism – but much better was hatred.

An important part of a good person's life is the restraint of hatred, and, in particular, the desire for revenge. Christ told us to love our enemies, one of the hardest and most important parts of a Christian way of life. There is a similar message in the teachings of the other great religions.

Nazism was founded on hatred: hatred of Jews, communists, Slavs – whoever was in the way or was simply (like the Jews and the gypsies) a convenient object of hatred.

Now, if you are prepared to lie by assertion, appeal to patriotism, conceal logic by emotion and cultivate hatred, you can make a very impressive and moving speech. Hitler's speeches produced mass hysteria, unquestioning loyalty to Nazism and the Führer himself, and an ultimate disaster for humankind.

It is important to realise that these techniques are far from dead in today's world. People are still encouraged to hate infidels and heretics, as the case may be. Workers are encouraged to hate bosses and corporations. Employers are encouraged to regard union leaders as communists. In a large body of American Republican opinion, 'liberal' is a term of derision. In Australia in recent years, political argument tends to deteriorate into mere slogan-chanting – for example: 'soft on border protection', 'soft on drugs' and so on.

In this book I seek to impart some of the concepts of persuasion, but it is important to realise that persuasion, the very oil of the democratic political machine, the basis for human progress, can be misused. The examples of Hitler and Goebbels should never be forgotten as fearful warnings of persuasion perverted.

To return to my criticism of the apparently successful speech, I was able to point to the so-called facts established by assertion, to the absence of logic, and, above all, to the appeal to the raw emotions of the audience. It was this appeal that produced the rounds of undeserved applause.

Persuasion is a noble art, but it must not be abused. I have illustrated this by the extreme examples of Hitler and Goebbels. But the boundaries of what is fair and reasonable and what is not are vague and far from clearly defined. Integral to persuasion is the understanding of the audience. At what point is it unfair or improper to appeal to the emotions, when such an appeal is often a fundamental part of the exercise?

I suggest that one should believe in the cause advocated, and be honest in the arguments advanced. Of course, sometimes it is the duty of an advocate to advance a cause, whether believed or not, as in the case of a barrister or solicitor. In these special cases, there are rules of advocacy designed to avoid abuses, and, to a considerable extent, these rules are effective. But a barrister speaks as an advocate and does not purport to believe in the cause advocated. In fact, for a barrister to say he or she does believe in the cause, even if it is true, is improper. Most juries appreciate this and are not impressed by barristers who break this rule. Nonetheless, a barrister must state the evidence accurately and honestly and use reasonable arguments.

Whether propounding one's own beliefs, or speaking as an advocate, arguments should be honestly expressed. Absence of logic or reason should not be concealed by appealing to raw emotion. It is necessary to be especially careful not to make a dishonest appeal to fear. For example, those in positions of influence have a grave responsibility to distinguish between appealing to fear of terrorists in order to defend against terrorism and appealing to fear of terrorists in order to stir up illogical alarm and political advantage. Sometimes the line of distinction is hard to define and the speaker may not care where it lies. It must be appreciated that appeals to fear can dispel logic, love, and mercy and expose the worst side of human nature. A master or mistress of persuasion bears (at times) a grave responsibility.

Ideas can be much more dangerous than most weapons of mass destruction. The foolish purveyors of gossip and slander, the poison-pen writers, are known as social menaces. How much more dangerous is the person who has acquired the art of persuasion and uses it maliciously, or even just carelessly. The more skilled one is in the art of persuasion, the greater is the duty to think carefully and persuade honestly. The good persuader is a trustee of his or her ability for the benefit of others. He or she must not use that ability irresponsibly.

3.

The basis of persuasion – the facts

IN ORDER TO ADVANCE a cause honestly and efficiently, it is first necessary to ascertain the facts. This is not always easy.

I have had the useful experience of being counsel assisting a number of Royal Commissions and inquiries and of being counsel for a party in such matters. In most of them, there had been previous court proceedings examining the issues at hand. From these inquiries emerged again and again instances of alleged facts being based upon surmisal or assumption rather than actual proof.

For example, when apparent knife or scissor cuts were found on Azaria Chamberlain's bloodstained jumpsuit, it was assumed that there had been human intervention because dingo teeth could not cut. When experiments were done using a kelpie dog and cloth to simulate the impact of a dingo's teeth on a piece of clothing it was revealed that the carnassial teeth of a dingo cut in a manner almost, if not completely, indistinguishable from a knife or scissors.

Another example of alleged facts being based upon assumption occurred in an arson case where the alleged accelerant was turpentine. I doubted whether it could be so used. So Jean, my scientist wife, and I did the experiment and found that it was quite a good accelerant, but with black smoke that would aid detection.

In the McDermott Royal Commission in 1951, one Lavers had been murdered outside his garage in the early morning of 5 September 1936 by persons in a particularly described car. McDermott was convicted of murder based upon his association with a 1926 Essex Tourer allegedly matching the suspect car. The suspect car had left 56 inch wheel tracks outside the garage. I appeared as junior to Jack Shand KC for McDermott at the Royal Commission inquiry into doubts as to the conviction. I proved that the motor journals of the time were wrong when they stated the wheel track of a 1926 Essex Tourer to be 56 inches. I measured many cars and eventually the track turned out to be 54 and $^7/_8$th inches, a vital fact that excluded the car in which McDermott was travelling from being the suspect car in which the murderers of Lavers would have been travelling.

I have been surprised to find that people have not done

a simple experiment to properly check the facts alleged in an argument. One rather vivid example is bloodstaining. A crime scene can give the impression of fearful injuries because of the extent of blood splashes. However, I have seen how large a mere teaspoon of blood appears when splashed on a flat surface.

These are all mere instances of forensic evidence. In the area of politics or social reform, and in the areas of protecting the environment, just to name a few areas where persuasion needs to be used, there is no substitute for careful study of the facts.

One rather extreme example of failure to check the facts was the lady who cherished a 'wild bush creature' which turned out to be a common brown rat. To do her justice she did ultimately make inquiries which revealed her blunder.

To advance a cause, there is a great temptation to adopt suitable 'facts' without further inquiry. This seems to occur often enough in politics. However if the 'facts' upon which a speech is based turn out to be errors, the speech may be destroyed and the cause may suffer. On the other hand, the careful, honest speaker whose 'facts' are always true facts will acquire a reputation for truth, which will command respect for his or her opinions. The desire to advance a cause should never be permitted to obscure the true facts, nor should mere laziness prevent one from making obvious and necessary inquiries.

Ascertaining the true facts on any question is often a long and tedious process. If there is an allegation that suits the argument, there is an obvious temptation to translate that allegation into fact. This is especially true in politics where the time available to find the true facts is limited and the need to speak is urgent. Furthermore, the parliamentarian cannot be sued for defamation for what he or she says in parliament. (Parliamentary privilege from being sued for defamation only applies to speeches in parliament.) Hence a convenient allegation frequently becomes an established fact in parliament.

This process is not the same as deliberate dishonesty, but the consequences may well be the same. Thus the wicked lies of Nazism were often repeated, even embellished, by normally good people who believed what they were saying.

The damage done by false allegations is so great that there is a duty on everyone to think and inquire before passing on information that may well be false. I suppose it is true to say that allegations of misconduct and evil about our fellow humans are only too common. Frequently these allegations are passed on without any inquiry as to their truth. If one pauses to reflect, this is unfair, and obviously can do great harm. Furthermore, if such allegations are made in a speech or writing, the person who made them can be liable for heavy damages for defamation. That is one of the consequences of careless preparation.

The other consequence is likely to be the destruction of the speaker's or writer's credibility. Fundamentally, effective ethical persuasion is founded on accurate fact finding and being caught out on a mistake as to the facts can be very serious. To be caught out on a lie can be disastrous.

Only a few persuaders are dishonest, but many are careless or lazy and fail to make proper inquiries before they advance a cause. Still more persuaders are neither dishonest nor particularly careless. However, as they warm to a cause and they look at the alleged facts with very prejudiced minds, subconsciously they believe what they want to believe.

One sees this lastmentioned phenomenon in the police practice of targeting a suspect. Having formed the view that a particular person is the perpetrator of the crime, the investigation proceeds on the basis of only looking for evidence against the target. Evidence that points away from the suspect is not so much ignored, rather it is not even noticed or recorded. Sometimes exculpatory evidence can be deliberately left out of the brief. In the bad days of not so long ago, the suspect might be 'loaded' or 'verballed'.

All this sounds dreadful, but many people do that sort of thing once they become dedicated to a political party or a cause. Many people believe the end justifies the means.

The truth is not always obvious. Usually thought and effort are required to reveal the truth. Often people are in a hurry.

But truth is precious. What is the use of learning the art of persuasion if the art is used to pervert the truth or to propagate lies? Fundamentally most of us want to do the right thing. We do not want to be dishonest; we do not want to spread untruths, even in good faith. Once we appreciate the dangers of failure to inquire, most of us will be careful.

There are a number of problems about ascertaining the truth. I suppose the first is simply laziness to which I have referred before. It is so easy to believe what one reads or is told, rather than make the necessary inquiries to ascertain the truth. The problem is accentuated by the modern media. Newspapers and TV news compiled quickly, often with an eye to creating sensation, are obviously dangerous. The internet contains an enormous amount of information with little in the way of a guide as to who vouches for the truth of the matters alleged. It is one thing to hear allegations, particularly allegations masquerading as news. It is another thing to repeat those allegations as if they were proven facts.

The second problem is even more important. Try as we may, we tend to believe what we want to believe. If allegations suit the cause, they soon become undoubted facts. If the allegations are repeated often enough by people who appear to believe them, they soon become established truth.

This links up with the third problem. One's listeners or readers tend to be complacent or busy. In either case, what they want is a brief, pithy message. On TV, these messages are often called 'grabs'. In their most effective form, they become slogans. A good slogan can win an election, particularly if it becomes a popular song. Thus the Liberal Party in 1951 adopted the song 'The only red we want is the red we've got in the old red, white and blue'. This was originally an American song against communism but did well in Australia's anti-communist elections in the 1950s.

The greatest slogans were those used for the election of Franklin D. Roosevelt as president during the dreadful depression of the thirties: 'There is Nothing to Fear but Fear Itself' and the song 'Happy Days are Here Again'.

In recent days in Australia, we hear such phrases as 'soft on border protection' to describe opponents of the Liberal Party or 'soft on drugs' to describe those who would reform the drug laws.

There is no doubt about the power of a pithy statement or slogan. The attraction of a slogan tempts perversion of the facts to create it, and suppression of the intelligence to accept it.

In busy modern lives, there is every temptation to cut corners, but in the long run there is no substitute for care and accuracy in stating the facts. Upon this accuracy depends the whole validity of the message sought to be conveyed.

Having said all this, I have to concede that it is very difficult at times to ascertain what are the true facts. The controversies in the politics of the USA, the UK and Australia as to whether there should have been a second war in Iraq demonstrate how difficult it can be to find out the true facts. This will often be so on questions of far less moment.

In the modern world, there is an enormous mass of alleged facts coming to the notice of any intelligent person. In many cases, it is hard to verify the truth of these statements. What I am advocating is a standard of perfection that is almost impossible to achieve. But the effort should be made.

There is one useful alleviation of the difficulty of alleged facts. It is wise to quote one's sources and authorities. Should these prove to be weak reeds, at least the speaker's credibility and integrity can survive when his or her alleged facts prove to be untrue.

In university circles, it is generally considered to be serious academic misconduct to use the words of another without stating the source. That, after all, is plagiarism. Where the alleged facts depend upon one or more sources, and cannot be checked as to veracity by the speaker, he or she is unwise to put those alleged facts forward as the simple truth without stating the source or sources.

If a speaker is honest, but proves to be mistaken through no fault on his or her part, then that speaker's integrity is maintained if the reason for the mistake is manifest. Integrity is a precious asset that should be preserved at all costs.

4.

Writing and speaking – the outline of a speech

THIS BOOK MAINLY CONCERNS the art of persuasion through speaking, so it is important to understand the limitations of the spoken message.

A reader who fails to understand or appreciate the significance of a sentence or two goes back and reads again. This frequently happens when the topic is complicated. With some authors fond of long words, it will even be necessary for the reader to consult a dictionary. A listener to a speech or a simple conversation will frequently miss something spoken, and if the bit missed was crucial, and is not repeated, the whole speech or conversation fails in its purpose.

A good way to appreciate this most important fact is to

compare one's memory of a newspaper article with that of a TV program on a serious topic. If the latter is well remembered, it is because the fundamental message or messages in the program have been vividly or constantly repeated.

In the law, this difference is very important in defamation cases. Years ago, the ABC telecast a program about the then New South Wales Attorney-General Mr McCaw and the illegal casinos in Sydney at that time. A basic error of fact was made by the author of the program as a result of which Mr McCaw was accused of being closely associated with the proprietors of the casinos. If one read a transcript of what was said in the program, there was a clear and false implied message that he was corrupt – a dreadful blunder by the ABC about an honest man. I appeared for the ABC in defamation proceedings resulting from the program and I was led by Jack Hiatt QC.

There was no way we could justify the words of that program. However, the significant words, which not unnaturally meant so much to Ken McCaw, passed in a flash to an ordinary audience when the program was screened. We insisted that the jury should not have a transcript of what was said, but should watch the program and assess the effect on an ordinary listener.

Even then, the position was not the same because the jury could watch and hear the program as often as it wanted to. The ordinary viewer and listener of a TV program or a speech hears it once only. Nevertheless, the jury understood our point and awarded very modest damages, $15,000, for what might well have been worth hundreds of thousands of dollars if the same words had been printed in a newspaper, with the same number of readers as there were viewers of the program.

Courts dealing with the written or printed word rightly presume that the reader will linger over sensational defamation statements. But the listener is unable to linger over a TV program or a speech.

All speakers need to keep this fundamental fact firmly in mind. If you want a listener to remember a speech, you must sum up the message or messages in simple propositions and the message must be repeated again and again so that it registers with the audience. The important feature of a speech is the impact of the message on the listener.

A very good example is one of history's great speeches, that of Martin Luther King shortly before he was assassinated. This message was the hope – nay, the certainty – of better understanding between black and white in America. This hopeful picture was depicted as the promised land of the Old Testament. Again and again he repeated the message 'I have seen the promised land'. It was a clever message because the listener would not only be unable to forget it, but would have to think about its significance.

Thus, if a speech is to have any lasting effect there must be a message, summarised into a fairly simple proposition, repeated and repeated, even if in different forms, until it has become embedded in the memories of the audience.

Some great parliamentarians have maintained that an effective speech will have only one message. I dislike rigid rules and I do not agree with this rule. I also think that there is a tendency to underestimate the intelligence of the average audience. I think that it is quite possible to have multiple messages. Much depends on the nature of the messages and the type of audience.

If the occasion is a lecture with people taking notes, the need for fundamental simplicity obviously recedes, but it should not be forgotten altogether. In modern parliaments, many speeches are intended to be read in *Hansard* rather than heard. In such cases, the necessary quorum pays little or no attention.

However, in the ordinary persuasive speech the message should be clear. Each step needs to be repeated and emphasised. If a step is missed and the listener is no longer following the reasoning, then that listener is lost unless a timely repetition or summary of what has been said before brings the lost listener back into the fold.

In this regard, it is important to illustrate the propositions in a speech (or, for that matter, in a written text). In a speech, the illustration not only retains the listener's attention, it ensures that the proposition is understood. One way of doing this is to use the illustration to introduce the idea rather than stating the idea followed by the illustration. For example, the economic theories behind the great financial bust of 1929 onwards are rather dull and difficult to follow, but the story of the great financial crash in the Great Depression is one that will hold any audience. The theory is more easily understood after describing the disaster.

Where a story is to be told, there is often a human touch that will bring it to life. Thus the story of the dismissal of the Lang government by the Governor of New South Wales Sir Phillip Game in 1932 comes to life if one describes the crowd that surged down Bent Street shouting 'The Governor has sacked Lang'. The story of the financial worries of the last days of the Lang government comes to life when it describes an ex-Light Horseman escorting a young treasury officer collecting debts to the government in actual cash, and delivering them to a treasury office swimming in coins and notes – collected to avoid a Commonwealth garnishee order over the State's bank accounts.

Sometimes the story can be so interesting that the speaker meanders from the main stream of the speech, but this is a minor error. If the audience is listening carefully, it can be easily brought back to the point.

The audience is likely to be both intelligent and

attentive. It is up to the speaker to make his or her points clearly, preferably early in the speech, and to leave a vivid message that will be remembered. Otherwise the speech may well be 'full of sound and fury', as Macbeth said about life, but it will be, in his words 'signifying nothing'.

Billy Hughes, the First World War Prime Minister of Australia, once complained about having to listen to a long dreary speech by a country member of parliament. His listener asked Billy, 'What was the speech about?' 'I don't know' was the reply, 'He didn't say'.

The first ingredient of a speech (or for that matter a piece of writing) is an object, a purpose. This seems obvious enough but how often does one say 'What was the point?'

There should be a clear object or purpose in the speech and that should become obvious during the speech.

Some speakers like to conceal the purpose, so that the audience is compelled to take part in a guessing game, and eventually the point of the speech is supposed to be seen as a great surprise. This technique has its dangers. I myself do not like it.

Sometimes the hidden message is realised prematurely by the audience and the build-up seems foolish. Sometimes the concealment of the message is annoying, and too often the revelation of a far from earth-shattering message comes as a dreadful anti-climax.

The hidden-message technique sometimes works, but beware of its failures.

I prefer the point of the speech to be quickly revealed and explained, and then it should be repeated in various ways so that at least the audience knows what the speech is about.

The theme – the object of a speech – is the most important and difficult part. If it is a good theme, the rest is so much easier. Even a funny after-dinner speech should have a theme, to which the jokes adhere, and which is, in fact, the source of most of the jokes.

The essential elements of a speech are the introduction; the stating, developing and illustration of the theme; and the conclusion.

In addition to the great parliamentarians I have mentioned before, there is the strong school of thought that says that there should be only one theme, but this really depends on the circumstances, the purpose of the speech, the audience and the time allotted. If care is taken with an audience, it can easily cope with more than one theme. There is a great tendency to underrate the audience's intelligence. Modern juries handle very complicated cases with numerous issues, and handle them well.

The modern juror often takes notes. Some other types of audiences also do. If notes are not being taken, there is a vital need to link everything together and this is harder with multiple themes. However, often one can have multiple themes as subdivisions of a main theme, and in such a case the whole can be fairly easily bound together.

Many speakers give a lot of thought to the introduction, and there is no doubt that a vivid opening can get audience contact and sympathy. An interesting story, a good quotation, a striking phrase, all of these can provide a good opening. Beware of long stories. Most audiences like you to come to the point.

Often not much thought is given to the conclusion, which is rather dull and lame as a result. The last impression is important. One should strive to sum up the preceding speech in words that will remain in the audience's mind.

A great example is Churchill's 'we shall fight on the beaches . . . we shall *never* surrender'. It was a desperate time in 1940 when many thought that further resistance to Hitler was useless. Churchill built up his speech by saying where 'we shall fight', on the beaches, in the towns, on the landing fields and so on as to build up to the great conclusion, 'we shall *never* surrender'. In four words he summed up and explained one of the great speeches of history.

A typical environmental-protection speech may conclude, 'Let your children, and their children, be able to see the beauty of this forest. Once destroyed it will never re-appear.' This conclusion would follow a theme developed as to how beautiful, how deserving of preservation are the trees and the wildlife of the particular area. By the time the conclusion is reached the audience wants to save the forest. The conclusion summarises and rams home the message of the speech.

It can be seen that the last sentences, in effect, summarise and repeat the theme of the speech.

Between the introduction and conclusion come the statement of and the development and illustration of the theme. This may well not be a padding to fill in time but the most interesting part of the speech. Here is the chance to develop arguments, to give interesting illustrations and here are the appeals to intellect and emotions that will hopefully convince the audience.

There are exceptions to everything, but most good speeches will adopt a structure similar to that which I have described. Attempts to escape altogether from this structure and be completely novel may succeed, but few do.

When planning a speech it is useful to ask two questions:

1. What am I trying to achieve?
2. Why should this audience listen to me?

The subject may interest you. It may not interest the audience unless you make it interesting.

Persuasion is not easy.

In particular, attention should be devoted to the second question. When preparing a speech, this concept should be ever present in your mind. There are enough boring speeches; do not add to their number.

5.

Aiming for the higher ground

ONE OF THE BIGGEST mistakes a barrister can make is to talk down to a jury. However ignorant juries may have been in the past, if they ever were, they are certainly intelligent and well informed today. As I have already stated, I have been impressed many times by the careful attention and the informed approach to their task displayed by juries, particularly since women became jurors. I was happiest to have a jury with approximately equal numbers between men and women, and thus the combined wisdom of the sexes acting in partnership.

In my time, I have talked to jurors about Marcus Aurelius guarding the Roman Empire on the German frontier. We all enjoyed the discussion, which was relevant to the criminals lurking on the edges of our brittle civilisation. Juries like to think, as do most people, if they are given the chance.

Juries readily appreciate the competing forces in a criminal trial, the need to convict the guilty and to free the innocent, the necessity for proof to be beyond reasonable doubt, lest an innocent person be convicted.

In my experience, if an appeal is made to the average citizen on the basis of some high principle, that appeal is more than likely to succeed. Why then do politicians aim their messages at the lowest common denominator in what they regard as an ignorant, greedy, selfish electorate? The 2004 federal election was a good example of this. Fundamentally, the so-called issues were of dollars and cents. Each party assumed electors were selfish and only thought about their own little monetary pockets, and nothing else.

Issues such as imprisonment without trial of Australians in Guantanamo Bay, children behind barbed wire for years in detention centres, true refugees imprisoned for years in such centres, Aborigines deprived and living in squalor, global warming, a threatened environment were ignored either in the main or altogether by both parties. What politician propounded a principle, not because it was a vote winner, but because it happened to be right and proper?

Australians despise their politicians and, in my

opinion, deservedly so. Elections have become pig-trough offers in which the electors are invited to wallow in monetary benefits provided out of their own tax payments. Electors are treated as stupid fools. Electoral propaganda is predicated on what the electors might be silly enough to believe, not on the facts.

Emotional abuse of the facts has been the fault of democracies since the days of Alcibiades of Athens in the Peloponnesian War, and even earlier. But we now have a well educated and, in my opinion, a fundamentally decent electorate. Why should not politicians appeal to its finer side, rather than to its greeds and hatreds?

As I have already stressed, the message propounded to public speakers and persuaders is to keep the message simple. This can be overdone. If a speaker is interesting and takes pains to explain, a modern audience can absorb very complicated concepts. This has been illustrated time and again in a legal context when ordinary jurors fully comprehended the evidence in commercial and company prosecutions. They required careful and clear explanations, and in return they gave intelligent attention, and produced accurate decisions.

This ability to concentrate attention and to understand, provided that care is taken to explain and make interesting, is vastly underestimated by those who address the public today, whether they be advertisers or politicians. It is so much easier to appeal to selfishness, greed and prejudice in the audience, rather than to aim for the higher ground.

Every great religion, whether Christian, Jewish, Muslim, Buddhist or Hindu, teaches the individual's duty to his or her neighbour, the message of love and mutual understanding. The further message is that if one has received a talent from the Great Creator, be it in this case of persuasion, then one is a trustee of that talent for the benefit of one's fellow citizens, if not of humankind generally, and has a duty to use it wisely and well.

Appeals to hatred and selfishness based on allegations created out of prejudice are easy to make and can be turned into very moving and effective speeches. The speaker will be cheered on and promotion and wealth may well come his or her way. But the speaker has betrayed the trust that goes with the gift of persuasion.

The advocates of the ultra-simple message will say that the vast majority of the public only understands simplicity and only as it concerns them. I disagree. People will listen and understand if a speaker takes the trouble to explain and simplify the complicated. Most people have a better side to their natures. If an appeal is made to the better side of the audience, it is only too happy, once it understands, to meet the speaker halfway.

People are not fundamentally bad, or even fundamentally selfish and greedy. It is true we all have these regrettable aspects of our characters, but we can rise above them. Most of us truly wish to do so.

A wealthy plutocrat can understand and sympathise with an underpaid worker or a deprived pensioner if the speaker takes the trouble to explain, to illustrate and to detail. It is not always easy but a good speaker can arouse the better feelings of the audience.

The overwhelming agreement of the Australian people in the 1967 referendum to aid Aborigines, the great march across the Sydney Harbour Bridge in support of reconciliation, and numerous demonstrations since, illustrate how ordinary people can be brought to sympathise with and want to help our Aboriginal brothers and sisters. But in 2004 neither political party considered that the dreadful problems of the Aboriginal community would interest the electorate. For myself, I refuse to believe, as the political spin-doctors do, that the electors' minds focus only on handouts of dollars for themselves. We all have souls, even if the political parties have sold their souls for votes.

What are the means whereby one reaches the hearts and minds of an apparently selfish audience?

The first concept in aiming for the higher ground is that one should not assume that the audience has no finer feelings – no aspirations for good. That assumption is almost invariably false. When one approaches an audience with the presumption that their hearts are governed by finer feelings, one is rarely disappointed. Most people are sympathetic to the troubles of others, most people aspire to the warm inner glow, and most people are not hypocrites.

The second concept is explanation. The more complicated the message, the more explanation it needs. It should be simplified but not at the expense of accuracy. All the time it should be made clear that the speaker is appealing not to the emotions so much as the fairness and perhaps compassion of the ordinary person.

Thirdly, interest must be maintained. Complicated concepts require illustration and repetition. Illustration is needed to explain and simplify the message. Repetition is necessary lest the speaker goes too fast for the audience.

Finally, when the other three points are achieved, one may appeal to the hearts of the audience for an emotional reinforcement of the logical conviction of their minds.

All this is not easy. It was easy for Hitler and Goebbels to attack the Jews or to thunder for war. It is easy to argue convincingly on false allegations playing on the worst side of the audience. It is easy to lower the audience. It is much harder to uplift them.

Sometimes a fine speech appears to have failed. In some of the press reports after Lincoln's Gettysburg address his political opponents derided what is now accepted as a wonderfully succinct and effective speech.

After that marvellous speech, he appeared to some, perhaps himself, to have failed. In fact, he had succeeded beyond his wildest dreams. This speech was not about money or prosperity. It appealed to the highest thoughts of its audience, and it succeeded.

People are often fools. We, in the Western World, fought two dreadful wars against each other, yet on both sides people demonstrated not merely bravery but tremendous disregard for self, and sacrifice for the community. In our present prosperous society, we tend to be selfish in a competitive economy. We excuse all sorts of wrongdoing as a means of supporting family prosperity. Yet people are basically good.

At Melbourne Zoo on a crowded Sunday, I saw a solid press of people at the edge of the monkeys' cage. One had to wait to see anything. Then a girl was wheeled in in a wheelchair. Immediately, without a word spoken, the crowd parted and the girl was pushed to a perfect view. That crowd was compassionate and unselfish. Those who stepped aside lost their positions and did not care.

One only needs to look around to see numerous people devoting themselves to charities and working tirelessly for good causes such as disabled persons. Even politicians are supported by numerous people who turn out for no reward but the satisfaction of doing what they think is right. In politics, among the grassroots supporters, one sees many unselfish, dedicated people, prepared to devote their time to a political cause without regard to personal reward. Some do party work for personal advantage, but most party workers seek no advantage, and receive none.

Many years ago I spent many hours on polling booths. There was a fellowship among us whether we were supporting Labor or Liberal. Most of us railed against the communists, but the camaraderie of at least one booth at which I worked included the communist lady, whom we liked despite her opinions. The point I make is that most of us had no prospect of reward, but felt a duty to participate in the political process by advancing the causes of our respective parties. This was illustrated most vividly by the many people who turned out to support Ted St John when he stood as an independent candidate for Warringah in 1969 after resigning from the Liberal Party. Whereas politics often enough reveal the unattractive side of those who participate, at the grassroots level it demonstrates how unselfish and public-spirited people can be.

Anyone who has the gift of persuasion, whether as speaker or writer, is able to improve society by the messages he or she may convey to the audience. As I have already mentioned, it is not true, even in politics, that that audience is mean, selfish, greedy and self-centred. It is an audience that can well be receptive to a message uplifting rather than degrading. It is an audience capable of understanding the problems of others and the problems of society generally, and, if inspired, anxious to do its part and its duty and even go beyond that. Crowds have been persuaded to riot, even to lynch unpopular persons. Crowds have been persuaded to clamour for war. The speeches to achieve these evil results are quite easy to make. Hitler was not a great speaker. He was merely a speaker without ethics who took the easy course. The speeches of Winston Churchill, however, were models of appealing to the finest aspects of patriotism and democracy.

So too, the speeches of Martin Luther King were not rabble-rousing. They were speeches inspiring an audience towards brotherhood of black and white, when there had been hatred and oppression. The audience's changed opinions were inspired by appealing to their finer feelings.

The finest addresses to juries have not been appeals to raw emotions, but rather appeals to their sense of fairness. Any good barrister speaks to a jury which he or she knows is doing its best to be fair, to do its duty.

Political rallies tend to go over the top. Nonsense is shouted out as though it is gospel, and the faithful clap and cheer. Political debates tend to look for votes prompted by prejudices. It is a pity that party planners and leaders do not simply work out what is right and take that to the electorate, not as a vote catcher, but as a message to uplift, not degrade the voters. This has happened in the past. In the late nineenth century Gladstone was a successful exponent of a campaign for what he thought was right, especially in 1884 when he sought justice for Ireland. There have been others since, but not enough, and not recently. Gough Whitlam has many detractors and he made mistakes, but he fought for what he thought was right, and for this he will be remembered as a great statesman.

I have used politics as a vivid example. The readers of this book will use their talents in many different spheres – company meetings, church meetings, club meetings, committee meetings, and council meetings. At any of these gatherings, it is a mistake to speak down to the audience, and it is ethically wrong to appeal to their worst natures, to their evil sides. Not only is it ethically wrong but it can backfire badly if someone feels that the speech appealing to the evil side of the listeners is itself, and for that reason, evil.

An appeal to the better nature of an audience, if it is appreciated and understood, can be enormously successful. The essential point to understand is that people have their good side and their bad side. The good side is much easier to find than many speakers imagine.

A good message should inspire and improve the audience and their world. That should be the real reason for learning the art of persuasion.

6.

The art of argument

MANY PEOPLE, PARTICULARLY THOSE in authority, such as some judges, prison warders, school principals and policemen, are firmly of the opinion that arguments are won by shouting down the opposition. Any experienced barrister will have come across this phenomenon more than once.

In 1974, when I was visting San Francisco, I read of two motorists whose vehicles collided with each other. One word led to another until one produced a pistol and shot the other in the chest. By good fortune, the bullet bounced off a rib and the victim survived. But as he was carried away he said, 'I reckon I lost that argument.'

There is a crucial difference between silencing and persuading the opposition, a difference that tends to be forgotten in hotel and domestic discussions, when people tend to assert rather than think. If you are in an argument purely for the purpose of letting off steam, by all means rant, rave and shout. You may feel better.

If you are in a position of authority, you may well be entitled to silence any would-be persuader who seeks to confuse you with facts.

However, if you are interested in passing on your ideas or in advancing a cause, shouting down the opposition will, in the long run, merely strengthen the counter-arguments. It is well to appreciate that your audience is likely to be well educated, and quite capable of distinguishing bluster from logic, and slogans from facts. In this regard, modern audiences may be different from some audiences in the past. There is a danger in copying old speeches.

In an ordinary discussion, it is good to let the other side have its say with questions by yourself aimed at understanding, not contradicting, the contrary arguments. The key to successful argument is to understand the listeners or audience as the case may be. Once one can appreciate the thoughts and motivations of the audience, the selection of suitable arguments to convince that audience is much easier.

In the good old days, barristers in criminal cases shouted and raved before juries. One barrister I remember well used to sob in front of them. (In those days, both barristers and jurors were all male and the standards of education were lower than today.) Such tactics are of dubious use today.

The modern jury, particularly once it became a mixture of ladies and gentlemen, is generally highly intelligent. If it contains any mugs, they usually follow the lead of the other jury persons. Jurors may take notes and, as often as not, are very familiar with the evidence, even in long cases. They readily understand complicated arguments. The key to failure is to treat the jury as slow or unintelligent.

The problem then is how to put forward one's arguments, or even how to choose which arguments to put forward. In ordinary discussions, or in arguments before judges and magistrates, one may well know the listener. However, in the courtroom the jurors are all strangers, and usually they, probably intentionally, appear inscrutable – at least, at first.

The object of the arguer should be to select arguments, and put them in such a way as to persuade the particular audience. In a court, however, the jury is unknown but one proceeds on the assumption that it is fairly representative of the community. Often one perceives that it has leaders who are taking intelligent notes and give an impression of being conscientious and capable. It is usually safe to assume that they, if won over, will convince the others.

Counsel addressing a jury will be seeking to put before them arguments that will persuade in a way that will appeal. It is essential to avoid arguments that may appeal to the arguer but not to the listeners. For example, if arguing that the accused was not in possession of cannabis, there is no need to say that cannabis use ought to be legalised and the prosecution is a waste of public money, even if you believe that.

In defending an accused on a charge of assault, it may be counterproductive to say that the victim provoked the attack, especially if the attacker is a much bigger man. If submitting an alibi by a long suffering wife, one might bear in mind that a jury will be likely to think that a wife's word on this topic is not worth much, so it is necessary to show that this particular wife would not lie for her husband. One would be foolish to say that no wife would lie for her husband. The effort should be to show that this particular one would not.

The need to be careful about some arguments is well illustrated by the difficulties of counsel defending men charged with sexual offences. It is surprising how often the perpetrator of sexual assault on a child claims that the child provoked his actions. To some limited extent this may even be true. However even to hint at the mere possibility of this having occurred is to invite the heavens to fall on you if you are counsel for the defence. I fear that many a wretch may have served further time on a longer sentence because his counsel was stupid enough to raise this forlorn argument. It is a good example of an argument that is like a red rag to a bull to the average judge or jury.

Even in the case of male sexual assaults on adult females the argument of provocation is a very dangerous one, which must be handled with great care, if put at all.

The point is that the argument that might appeal to you may simply close the listener's mind against you. Therefore you must either use a different argument or dress up the difficult argument in a more attractive way.

In other words, you are not trying to convince yourself. You are trying to convince others. This point emerges much more clearly in the situation where the argument takes place in a one-on-one situation and the person to be convinced is known to the persuader.

Of course, many arguments are valid and effective for any audience, but there are still many ways and means of making them persuasive to the particular audience. Choosing examples familiar to a local jury is a common feature of counsel operating in country towns. However one can interest juries in quite extraordinary topics if the story has merit.

I propose to develop these ideas, firstly in relation to one-on-one discussions and then for wider and larger audiences.

Many good speakers to large audiences give the impression to each listener that he or she is being addressed personally.

Persuasion is usually envisaged as a speech or a written submission to a large audience. Yet, most commonly, persuasion is an important part of daily human contact between individuals, whether simply in a social context or for serious business or political purposes. It is from this one-on-one conversation that the larger effort to reach a wider audience is developed. A study of this type of persuasion is the key to the whole art of argument.

Perfect examples of one-to-one persuasion occur every day in our courts when the advocate for the defendant tries to persuade a judge or magistrate to be lenient to his or her client for some criminal offence. It may be merely to reduce a fine for a traffic offence. It could be to reduce the term of imprisonment for murder. The defendant may have been found guilty after a trial. Much more frequently, he or she has pleaded guilty. The success or failure of the attempt to persuade the court to be lenient often appears vividly enough in the judgment on sentence.

Many years ago, when I was a young barrister, I appeared before the late Judge Berne, known generally for good reason as 'mad Freddie'. My client had been given a bond by His Honour a year or so before in respect of a stealing offence. He had narrowly escaped gaol then and had been solemnly warned that if he offended again he would be imprisoned. As is too often the case for young offenders, my client had now offended again.

I did not expect to have an easy time, but as soon as I announced my appearance His Honour in a far from quiet voice immediately said, 'Mr Porter, I promised your client that if he offended again he would go to gaol.' Then, almost pointing his finger at me, he roared, 'Mr Porter, are you trying to make me out to be a liar?' I reeled back at this.

Probably it was more by good luck than skill that I did the right thing. I just stood there and looked humble and His Honour went on and on. Occasionally I said, 'Yes, your Honour'; very rarely I said, 'but, your Honour', until I realised that at the pace he was going he was going to run out of ideas. All I had to do was stay on my feet and he would change his tack. Since he had exhausted himself on the topic of imprisoning my client, he was likely to veer around to yet another bond. And so it transpired, my contribution being limited to 'yes, your Honour' and 'but, your Honour' and finally 'if your Honour pleases' when my client left the court, a lucky man.

I can remember a similar instance of a judge talking himself around when Jack Hiatt QC led me in a case in Canberra involving dredging pebbles from the Murrumbidgee River. (We were for the dredger who was alleged to have dredged gravel belonging to Lanyon Pty Ltd, a riverside owner. This was a civil case for damages.) Mr Justice Smithers was a very genial, pleasant and able judge but he could be quite loquacious and he was on this occasion. In fact, Mr Hiatt's submissions were cut off by a long speech from the bench showing how our case simply had to fail. Jack did his best to get our points across but was simply talked down. It is easy for a judge to do this, and it looked as though our case was history. Jack looked at me and said, 'Is there any point in going on?' and I replied, 'Just keep standing; he will talk himself around.'

So Jack kept standing, for a long time as it turned out, saying little more than 'but, your Honour' for about half an hour. In the end, Mr Justice Smithers had changed his mind completely and his decision was in our favour.

I suppose the lesson from these two cases is that it may sometimes pay to let the other party have his or her complete say. Only then will he or she contemplate a change of mind.

In everyday life, and in courts, one not infrequently finds two firmly cemented minds confronting each other, neither side prepared to concede even the slightest point. Yet in many, if not most, of these cases, if one party simply stays quiet and lets the other have a full run until he or she has nothing further to say, a useful, sensible discussion may then result.

The big feature of exercises in persuasion is that assertion is no substitute for reasonable argument.

The key to successful persuasion in such situations is to understand the person to be persuaded. Failure to do so may lead to disaster.

Some years ago, there was yet another army initiation ceremony. This was a rather nasty one involving interference with private portions of the body, such as to shock the average judge. For some reason, it went before a District Court judge instead of an army court martial.

Counsel for the young soldiers made a serious tactical error. He suggested that such occurrences in the army were only to be expected, along the 'boys will be boys' line of thought. The judge was most unfavourably impressed and sent all the soldiers to gaol. I came into the case after that in order to try to get them out of gaol, on appeal.

Acting for the first time in a case at the appeal court level has some similarity to a surgeon digging for an appendix after the first operation has failed. One has to live with all the consequences of the previous attempt. This case was one in which I would have to eat large quantities of humble pie.

So, when I appeared in the Court of Criminal Appeal, I expressed great horror at what my clients had done and the judges could not wait to agree with me. Thus public disapproval for the stupidity of young idiots was loudly and forcefully expressed. Action is followed by reaction and in no time I was receiving a sympathetic hearing when I pointed to my clients' prior good characters, their youth, and so on. It soon appeared that it was unnecessary to send them to gaol and they were all freed on bonds to be of good behaviour.

The lesson of all this is clear enough. To persuade another, you must have regard for what he or she thinks. Your own ideas may simply operate to provoke a counter-reaction.

Before this lastmentioned case, I had had a somewhat similar matter in which I appeared for a young soldier who, while on leave, got drunk, broke a shop window in a country town and helped himself to some goods, cigarettes as I remember it. We drew Wal Redapple, a stern judge, one-time crown prosecutor, of conservative views and likely to be enraged by a young hoodlum's smash-and-grab enterprise. In these circumstances, drunkenness may be a convincing reason, but it fails dismally as an excuse.

I knew His Honour quite well when we were fellow barristers. I liked him. He was a returned serviceman who was proud of the fact.

This was in the middle of the Vietnam War, a most unpopular war in which returned servicemen often received little credit and much abuse. My client was on leave from service in Vietnam. So I opened up as follows:

'Your Honour will remember how, after the war, returned servicemen who got into trouble with the criminal law could appeal to their past war service as a reason for leniency. But Vietnam is an unpopular war. Perhaps service in the jungles of Vietnam is no basis for leniency when the war is unpopular.'

His Honour: 'It is in my court, Mr Porter.'

And so it was. My client escaped gaol and His Honour recommended that the army should receive this erring soldier back into its ranks, and he was so received. So far as I know, he went on to make something useful of his life.

But what would have happened if I opened up by saying that soldiers on leave could be expected to get drunk, and what was a broken shop window and a few cigarettes? I may well have thought that, but no self-respecting court purporting to protect the community could possibly express such ideas as acceptable.

The lesson is the same. The argument that counts is not the one that appeals to you; it is the one that convinces the listener. Of course, often your mind will coincide with that of the listener, but this conclusion should not be presumed. It should only be reached after much thought.

I have often heard advocates say little more to the sentencing judge than 'I ask your Honour to give my client a bond' without any real reasons added. This is, of course, shocking advocacy. In fact, even in a case that may well merit leniency, a first offender of otherwise good character, to presume leniency is to tempt fate. One should seek leniency as a favour from the law, not as a matter of routine.

When one's client has really blotted his or her copybook and has little in the way of excuse, a good advocate looks carefully and looks hard to find matters in his or her client's favour.

Of course, he or she can get credit for a prompt plea of guilty if that is the case. Youth and prior good character are matters of relevance and the Crimes (Sentencing Procedure) Act prescribes numerous relevant matters. Obviously all possibly relevant matters should be checked, but success may well depend upon appropriate stress and the 'dressing up' of relevant matters.

Careful thought and careful expression are the keys to success. I remember, as a very young counsel, hearing Fred Vizard, a dedicated early Public Defender, appearing for a man with a terrible criminal record – and he was doing the same things again. What could be usefully said?

'Your Honour,' said Fred Vizard. 'My client obviously has a very bad record, but he has served his gaol terms for those offences, he has taken his punishment; any sentence now imposed should not punish him again for those offences.' Fred was a fine man who gave his best for clients who were often quite hopeless and almost beyond redemption.

If one knows that the judge is a rugby union enthusiast, and many are, it is worth dredging up any achievements of your client in that respect. In my experience, old soldiers were often impressed by young soldiers.

Saying something useful was often difficult. I always checked my client's criminal record because very frequently they lied to you about their antecedents. I remember once asking Joe Morris, a famous gaol recorder of the old days, about my client's record. 'He's done everything,' said Joe (which was fairly true). 'Well,' I said, 'he's never made a graven image.' 'That'll be next,' said Joe.

For such clients, it was hard to find redeeming features. One had to talk at length with the person and his friends and family. This could take a long time. More often than not, something useful emerged.

Care needed to be taken with submissions. Drunkenness is a self-induced incapacity. It may explain a crime, but these days few people regard it as an excuse. In fact, some people think it makes the offence worse. The same applies to drug addiction, but if one can show that the culprit is now on a firm program of rehabilitation, it may not be in the community's interest to send him or her to gaol.

One must always keep in mind what the judge or magistrate is thinking.

I appeared once for a young man found in possession of quite a lot of cannabis, which he said was for his own use. On my advice, rather reluctantly accepted, he undertook to the court that he would not smoke cannabis again. He got off with a fine. Later, another young man arrested at the same time on similar facts was sent to gaol. His counsel apparently made the mistake of submitting that it was 'only cannabis'.

The fundamental point is that the argument that convinces others is not necessarily the one that convinces you. In fact, you may be out of step with the person you need to convince.

The same concepts applicable to persuading a judge apply to ordinary persuasion in domestic and business life. One need not be as humble as an advocate before a judge, but politeness pays. It is a good idea to try to ascertain the thinking of the person you wish to persuade. Therefore, if possible, let the other one speak first, listen carefully and understand.

It is usually much easier to persuade a single person than a group, but it depends on the personnel of the group. Appellate courts usually consist of three, five, or sometimes seven judges. Appellate judges are normally persons of brilliant intellect, who are neither overly patient nor unduly modest. Sometimes such judges reveal their own thinking on the issues and counsel then has a firm basis for argument. Sometimes the advocate addresses silent stony faces.

Sir Garfield Barwick, in my opinion and that of many others, argued with tremendous ability before appellate courts. He simplified the complicated, and his arguments were convincing. His addresses were interesting, and often entertaining. Yet Sir Owen Dixon, when Chief Justice of Australia, secretly regarded his arguments as of next to no assistance to the court (Phillip Ayres 'Owen

Dixon'). I have appeared several times before Sir Owen Dixon, who was noted for his pleasant manner in court. What must he have secretly thought of me?

I found that the High Court and the New South Wales Court of Appeal were difficult courts for an advocate, but a good argument, reasonably presented, usually had a good reception. In the main, the questions argued were as to the legal principles applicable to the cases in question. Such arguments are carefully based on authority and principle and far removed from the addresses made to a jury.

Submissions to an appellate court are not all that far removed from submissions made to a company board, a committee, or a local council. One has to put arguments before a body of intelligent persons who may have very strong opinions.

I remember once arguing before the Court of Appeal and my main argument was continuously rebuffed by the court. Instead, the judges thrust on me another argument in my favour, which eventually won the appeal for me – for their reasons, not mine. The other side then appealed to the High Court.

The High Court then thrust upon me my original argument. I said that I had tried it on the Court of Appeal, which had rejected it. 'Try it on us,' replied Sir Garfield Barwick, then Chief Justice. Of course I did, and won that appeal for my original reasons.

This is typical of arguing before such a body. Ideas, good ideas, will come back to you from the bench of judges, the board of directors or the committee, as the case may be. Usually you will have very little time to decide whether to adopt ideas in your favour. Yet you must be very careful about abandoning or putting to one side carefully prepared arguments, in favour of adopting a new argument that may or may not be sound.

Arguing before such a body usually has the advantage that one is told how those to be persuaded are thinking. One may shape and mould one's arguments accordingly, subject to the possibility that there is division of opinion between members of the bench or committee.

Where there is such a division, it may be very dangerous indeed to adopt an argument from one judge or committee member if that helpful person turns out to be in the minority.

Probably a good general rule is to prepare your argument carefully, adapt it to comments, but be very careful about abandoning your careful preparation for a new idea.

In the position I have described, the person putting up a submission is often interrupted and is not infrequently subjected to adverse, even rude, comments. Particularly to a bench of judges, it is wise to stay polite even when the comments from the bench are far from polite. Above all, one must not lose one's equilibrium, still less one's temper.

It can be an exhilarating process, even if at times not so pleasant.

When addressing such a body of persons, it is likely that one or more will know much more about the subject under discussion than you do. This frequently occurs. In fact, it seems to have been more or less inevitable in the case of Sir Owen Dixon. Nevertheless, you have prepared and concentrated upon the particular submissions you are arguing. It is wise to keep close to those.

I remember once in the High Court as a junior counsel I argued a criminal appeal from New Guinea. At that time, the High Court was the only appeal from a New Guinea conviction. The case involved a manslaughter conviction of my client who had kicked his wife, bursting her abnormally enlarged spleen so that she died as a result. He had no idea that her spleen was abnormally enlarged.

Was this an 'accident' under the Queensland Criminal Code which was the law applying to New Guinea? I made the mistake of referring to the history of manslaughter. One of the judges, Sir Victor Windeyer, was a brilliant legal historian and in no time had me completely out of my depth. He expounded the history of homicide back to medieval times. I floundered. He was a gentleman and let me off lightly, but it was a good example of the dangers of wandering off the carefully prepared material into areas where the tribunal might well be much better informed than you are.

Appeal judges are usually brilliant persons, and even if not so brilliant, are not noted for modesty. They are, as a kind, not averse to displaying their own learning or peremptorily contradicting counsel making submissions. Worst of all, some love to make long dissertations preventing counsel putting any submissions at all to the court. They are difficult persons to persuade. Yet the fundamental rules apply. Do not put arguments in a way that will provoke and repel; do not put arguments that of themselves will not convince but only provoke (even if you agree with the arguments yourself); mould your arguments so as to appeal to the recipients; and, of course, be very well prepared.

Addressing an appeal court is a task for experienced counsel, and certainly it is a trap for ambitious amateurs. Nevertheless, the cut and thrust of argument and the intelligent examination of propositions is stimulating.

As always, it is essential never to lose one's temper and important to try to avoid being thrown off balance.

The jury is often an enigma. Jurors say nothing, except for an occasional written question to the judge. In recent years, each juror has a number only. Nothing is known as to names, addresses or occupations of jurors. You are addressing twelve completely unknown people. Yet, as the trial progresses, smiles, nods and note-taking may give some clues as to an individual's thinking.

Usually, though, the advocate knows nothing as to how

the jury is thinking. Obviously in a strong Crown case, defence counsel may fear the worst, just as with a strong defence case there is room for optimism.

Addressing the jury, counsel will normally strive for eye contact with the whole jury and, as the address proceeds, careful observation will often reveal agreement or disagreement among the jurors. It is not an easy exercise. When attempting to persuade a person one knows well, arguments may be selected to suit that person, but when addressing twelve jurors, one is addressing twelve minds, some of which may drastically differ from the others. Some jurors may like an argument and others may be repelled by it.

When addressing any group of persons, the object should be to produce convincing arguments and express them in a persuasive way. When the audience is unknown, one has to argue in the dark to some extent. One should avoid provocative statements likely to offend one or more of the group, that is, unless such statements are necessary to develop the main theme and cannot be avoided. Then it is necessary to be tactful and to choose words carefully.

Of course, some arguments – in fact, many arguments – have universal appeal and are undoubtedly valid. Nevertheless, even for these, care must be taken lest careless expression spoils the effect, or raises unnecessary opposition.

When one comes to a large meeting, it is a good idea to try to ascertain the type of persons present. Apt illustrations that appeal to the particular audience are very effective. Expressions that might offend can be avoided. Friendly contact can be achieved. However, one should not pretend to false feelings just to please a particular audience. Not only is it unethical, but hypocrites are usually found out in this situation.

What I have been stressing in this chapter is the importance of adapting your argument to the audience. This does not mean moulding false arguments. Rather it means selecting from possible arguments and, perhaps more importantly, careful expression of the arguments chosen.

For example, if a jury is trying a prominent politician for a criminal offence, and this does happen, defending counsel would be wise to avoid party political attacks. The jury persons may belong to the party attacked. Rather, the appeal should be to the complete impartiality of the jury, so the accused will receive a fair trial regardless of the party loyalties that some jurors may have. On most occasions, this appeal is well received and acted on by the jury.

For example, at a public meeting to save a public reserve from undesired development, care should be taken not to make an unfair attack on a particular councillor. A vigorous defence of that councillor in reply to that attack may defeat the whole purpose of the meeting. On these occasions, it is often thought that vigorous, fiery personal attacks are called for, but more often than not they are counter-productive. This does not mean that the speaker should not be vigorous and emotional, but personal attacks should be avoided if at all possible.

Arguments that leave no honourable retreat for the opposition are obviously to be avoided. Life rarely grants the satisfaction of overwhelming and utter defeat for one's opposition, but the attempt to secure that result can easily turn victory into defeat at the hands of a cornered opposition.

The extreme statement, the extreme stand, the stonewall approach, all have their attractions. They attract cheers and applause but they also raise unnecessary opposition. People can change their minds after able persuasion but few minds change in the face of insulting or bullying tactics.

If you want cheers from your side, and no more, then what I have said will carry little weight. If you want to persuade the opposition, if you want to carry the maximum possible majority, then you will treat your opponents with manners and respect and persuade them with reason.

If you were once a successful team debater, or an enthusiastic member of the audience at such debates, it is very important to appreciate the limits of such a debate. Many 'points' are scored, opposing speakers are humiliated, sarcastic comments bring loud cheers from the audience, but who changes their minds? Who is persuaded?

Contrast these debates with the discussions of a committee or a company board of directors where a quiet, carefully phrased speech can often change the whole course of proceedings. Even in these small bodies, speakers can become emotional or personal, but the careful persuader will usually carry the day.

7.

Finding the issue

ALTHOUGH ARGUMENTS ARE OFTEN pursued at great lengths over trifling details, even in court cases, serious disputes are concerned with issues. These issues are often concealed by disputes as to details.

In the case of Lindy Chamberlain, there were innumerable conflicts over matters that concealed the main issue – namely, did Lindy kill her baby Azaria, *not* did a dingo take the child?

There were days spent trying to decide whether tears on the baby's jumpsuit were cuts made by human hands, or whether they were dingo tears. However, even if the former were the case, the real issue was not did a dingo make the tears, but rather did the Chamberlains do so?

The clothes were found five days after the Chamberlains left Ayers Rock. There was no evidence that the Chamberlains put the clothes where they were found at Maggie's Springs, and it would have been difficult indeed for them to have done so without being seen. Seven days had passed since the baby disappeared, yet the blood-stained clothing had not been widely scattered by feral predators common in the area. The clothes were dry when found even though it had been raining earlier in the day.

Assuming the tears in question were cuts made by human hands, the only relevant issue was did the Chamberlains cut the jumpsuit. Yet at the trial it seemed to be assumed that only they could have done so, if the clothes were in fact cut.

That is a complicated example but numerous people arguing over this case said, 'The clothes were cut, therefore the baby was killed by Lindy.' Why? It was said that the clothes were placed by the Chamberlains near a dingo den and cut so that it would appear that a dingo took the baby. Yet none of the white residents, including the chief ranger and his deputy, knew of the situation of that particular den. One might add that if there was an intention to frame the dingo, much more cutting and tearing might have been expected.

The trouble with the purported issue – murder or dingo – was that it concealed the real issue: whether or not Azaria was murdered by Lindy. Thus cutting by human hands, not dingo, was assumed to be evidence of her guilt.

In legal cases, the path to good advocacy and justice is to find the real issue. This is so also in everyday disputes. People argue to no purpose because they fail to find the real issue of their dispute.

When I was a very young man, as a member of the Liberal Party I was part of the minority in that party opposing the attempt to ban the Communist Party. The debate within the party was only part of a much wider debate, eventually resolved by a constitutional referendum in 1951. The Menzies government only narrowly lost this referendum proposal. It took some time for a significant issue to emerge in this political controversy – namely, who was going to be banned. What was to be the definition of a communist? If only a member of the Communist Party was to be affected, then the underground communists would continue their activities unaffected. One could simply resign from the party and pursue communist activities unofficially. So a detailed definition of communist was put forward in the bill under consideration, which many thought, with reason, would pick up most socialists and even mild social reformers. It was probably only the doubts on this question that lost the referendum, not the broad question of political liberty for everyone. Those opposing the referendum picked up this problem of defining a communist and used the doubts and problems arising from the proposed definition to great advantage.

Much more recently, in November 1999, a referendum on the question of whether to continue with the monarchy or make Australia a republic was completely frustrated by a wrangle as to how the new president was to be elected. The republicans split on this question and the referendum to abolish the monarchy, as it applied to Australia, was defeated because many republicans did not agree with the proposal put forward in the referendum to elect the president by a two-thirds majority of a joint sitting of the federal parliament. Thus the main issue was frustrated by the subsidiary question. The referendum to get a true answer should have contained two questions:

1. Are you in favour of a republic?
2. Are you in favour of the specified method of electing the president?

Although the government was accused of political trickery over this referendum, the legal situation was that the abolition of the monarchy could only be achieved by a referendum amending the Constitution that would have to provide a method of electing the president. If many republicans preferred to defeat that referendum rather than defer to the proposed method of election, then the referendum would be lost, and the monarchy would stay.

It is often difficult to define the issue because there is usually more than one issue and the issues are often intertwined. In such cases, there is all the more reason to ascertain and define those issues.

My good friend Vic Hall, to whom I have referred previously, once startled a meeting of Rostrum members by defining the three steps necessary to solve a problem:

1. Appreciate that there is a problem.
2. Define precisely what the problem is.
3. Solve the problem.

At the third step, the audience laughed, but I did not. The whole point is that the solution of a problem is usually not hard; it is the defining of the problem that is more difficult. Once the definition is perfected, the solution is usually obvious.

Disputes are not precisely the same as problems, but there is a close similarity. If the issue or issues in a dispute are ascertained and precisely defined, the dispute either solves itself or is at least much easier to resolve.

In ordinary life, and often in court cases, arguments are usually about irrelevancies or fringe issues. How does one ascertain the real issue or issues? Before one enters into an argument, the ideal is to ascertain the real issue by mental analysis and calm consideration of the facts. Only occasionally will there be more than one real issue.

Thus in the case of banning the Communist Party the real issue was: was it necessary to sacrifice a substantial amount of freedom in order to preserve Australia from the danger of communism? That was the only real issue but the subsidiary questions that arose from that issue were numerous, such as how do you define a communist, how much restriction is necessary to control communists, will the proposed restrictions work and be effective or will they engender sympathy for communists? Yet all these questions are really only arguments one way or the other about the main issue.

In all cases of proposed change, the problems involved in the change may be strong arguments in favour of the status quo.

If one considers the political problem of the old growth forests in Tasmania, the issue might be defined as: does the obvious benefit of retaining the forest outweigh the obvious hardship imposed on the timber workers, and financially on the whole state, by destroying a profitable industry? The problem becomes a balancing act and the argument should be resolved by a careful analysis of the advantages of retaining the forest – for example, tourism, environmental protection, the impossibility of replacing such forests – against the disadvantages – for example, jobs lost, financial benefits lost in a state with a lack of industries and employment opportunities. Those arguing for the trees might suggest that wood-chipping is a poor return for non-renewable assets, that tourism needs the forests, and so on. Those arguing against might point to vast forest areas already preserved, to towns and workers dependent on the timber industry, and so on. Tree preservers arguing to timber workers might stress the alternative employment offered by tourism and compensation available for lost jobs. Timber industry arguments to tree preservers would stress the area already preserved. In such a difficult dispute, using names such as 'chain-saw vandals' and 'tree-huggers' for opponents contributes only heat, not enlightenment. This is essentially a difficult dispute that can only be solved by arguments that fully appreciate the opposing viewpoint and do not purposely antagonise.

In court cases, many a case is lost by taking up side issues, or dead-end issues, rather than keeping attention always on the main issue. So it is with all disputes. Argument should concentrate on the main issue; side issues should only be used to pursue the main issue.

Before becoming involved in an argument and throughout the subsequent discussion, one should keep asking oneself, 'What is the point I am trying to make? Have I become diverted into a side issue? Has the real point been lost?' The ascertainment of the real issue can be a greater task than arguing the case when it is found. For prepared addresses, careful and intelligent preparation should first be aimed at this crucial question.

In ordinary conversation, or perhaps in committee discussion, it not infrequently happens that an argument, quite heated in nature, suddenly breaks out. A wise participant, or especially a chairperson, if there is one, will seek to ascertain precisely what is the dispute. Not infrequently there has simply been a misunderstanding between persons. Of course, the further the argument goes, the greater the heat, and the less chance there is of ever ascertaining the real issue.

For a prepared speech, the speaker should first ascertain the issue and address it; otherwise there is no purpose served for the speech. Even for an impromptu speech it is necessary to detect the issue.

It often happens that the main issue is clear enough but the subsidiary issues are all important. For example, in an Australian election, the main issue is clear enough, the choice between the two major parties, Liberal or Labor. The subsidiary issues are possible reasons for supporting one party or the other, such as better financial management, more generous social services, more or less aid to private schools, better defence services, more efficient government, a more humane immigration policy, rural subsidies, and so on. An examination of past elections shows quite clearly that the winning party tended to pick one or two issues that it thought would appeal and stress it or these. The party's policy may cover many issues; only some will be debated at the election and only one or two will be the issue or issues that may decide the election.

Taking another example, imagine yourself on a

company board or a council and there is a motion to dismiss a senior employee. Here, the main issue is clear enough: to dismiss or retain the services of the person in question. There may be many reasons to retain that person and probably only a few to dismiss him or her. The protagonists on either side will do best to select and stress one or two of the subsidiary issues; for example, inefficiency of the employee, the long service of the employee, the employee's inability to find other employment, the employee's past achievements, whether the employee can be easily replaced, whether a new employee would give better service, and so on.

Before you, as a board member or councillor, make up your mind you will weigh these matters up and reach a conclusion. You will do so by selecting usually only one or two of the subsidiary issues which convince you. Normally you will then stress these to the rest of the board or the council. Very often discussion will centre on only one of these subsidiary issues. Picking the right one can be the path to success, but, as I have stressed before, the issue that convinces you will not necessarily be the one that appeals to the others.

It may be that you will select as the 'key' issue one matter which will appeal to the others, even though it was not the matter which convinced you. More probably you state the issue which persuaded you in a way which will appeal to the others.

The whole point of this chapter is that you must find the issue and speak to the issue. You do not speak just to hear your own voice, or to make a great sound, or to fill in time. If your object is to persuade you must find the issue (or issues) which will persuade and develop it (or those).

8.

Simplification

THERE IS A GREAT attraction in understanding the complicated. One of the late Sir Garfield Barwick's greatest assets was his ability to simplify. This is not the same as finding the issue. Once the issue has been located and precisely defined in the mind of the persuader, it and the questions raised by it must then be expressed in terms that the audience can understand. Sir Garfield had the gift of reducing complicated legal concepts into simple, readily understood statements.

Once the audience feels it understands something difficult to comprehend, it feels real gratitude to the speaker, and will readily accept persuasion by that speaker.

However, simplification is not nearly as easy as it might

at first appear. To reduce the complicated to the simple may well be at the expense of the truth of the final proposition. The object of the exercise of persuasion is not mere simplification; it is simplification without distortion.

It is sometimes said that the test of an expert is whether he or she can explain matters pertaining to the relevant expertise in simple terms. The means to simplification are thorough knowledge of the subject and a great deal of thought.

There is no doubt that many experts hide imperfect knowledge behind long words that only their fellow experts understand. I found that in cross-examination of experts, insistence that each long technical word be translated often produced remarkable results. This was especially so with some psychiatrists. What sounded very impressive in technical words became quite ridiculous when translated into simple English.

I, for one, have a healthy mistrust of experts who use many long technical words to laypeople. However, one must appreciate that many audiences are impressed by technical words that they cannot understand. As W.S. Gilbert wrote (in the Gilbert and Sullivan opera 'Patience'):

> If this young man expresses himself in terms too deep for me,
> Why, what a very singularly deep young man this deep young man must be!

Many people tend to regard technical words as proof of competence in an expert. The medical profession has a whole language contained in medical dictionaries. If a doctor says 'That is a bruise', the patient is unimpressed, but if the doctor says 'You have a haematoma', it is felt that value is being received for money.

So it may well be that an expert's audience expects words that it cannot understand. Who would believe an economist who spoke in simple terms?

Probably the best approach to persuading an audience is to use the occasional technical word and immediately translate it on the way.

The same applies to acronyms. These days we are smothered in acronyms and only understand a few. The use of these is probably more irritating than the use of technical words. If a forensic scientist refers to NIFS without explanation, few will understand that the reference is to the National Institute of Forensic Science. The best approach is to use the full name first then apply the acronym. Sometimes, if it is important, it may be wise to translate the acronym more than once. It is easy to forget the first translation.

The main point is that the theme of the speech should be reduced to a simple sentence or sentences that are readily understood, but that accurately present the theme, no matter how complicated. Normally this should not be all that difficult in a persuasive speech.

However, expertise does frequently enter into persuasive speeches. For example, if the theme is to permit (or limit) stem-cell research, there must be some explanation of stem cells and what occurs in stem-cell research. If the theme is to encourage more government borrowing to improve infrastructure and facilities for the public, the arguments will be based on expert economics.

In such cases, the use of quickly translated technical terms can inspire confidence in the speaker's expertise, but it is a delicate tight-wire exercise. On the one hand, the audience wants evidence that the persuader knows his or her subject; on the other hand, there is a resistance against being 'blinded with science'.

One must beware of the use of statistics. As the saying goes, there are lies, damn lies and statistics. Only a very unsophisticated and poorly educated audience should be impressed by statistics, which are widely used to excuse and deceive. The attraction of statistics is that they are initially so persuasive and impressive. An audience, however, is likely to think further and use its intelligence. The accuracy of statistics depends very much upon the definition of terms used.

Thus ninety per cent of all women have been sexually abused. This statement may be true if you have a wide enough definition of 'sexually abused'. The unstated definition behind the ninety per cent may include a glimpse of a 'flasher' or even hearing nasty words. Thus this particular example may be fifty per cent, ten per cent or ninety per cent, depending on the definition of 'sexually abused'.

Even the Bureau of Statistics depends upon samples obtained from often unwilling informants who are subject to statutory compulsion to answer questions to which they do not know the answers otherwise they will be fined. Most statistics are obtained by questions to sample informants. If the questions are vague or misleading, or if the sample is not fairly reflective of the whole, the statistics are little better than confidence tricks. I speak from personal experience. I received several demands, not requests, for information. Some years ago, the Bureau published statistics as to the income of Sydney barristers, which appeared to be, and almost certainly were, ridiculous, based, I suppose, upon a sample of inaccurate answers from persons such as myself. Such would come from both the answers and the selection of the sample.

Every government minister or senior civil servant has figures and statistics available to explain any matter causing concern. Thus any complaint is answered with a statistic.

Statistics are suspect, indeed. Their use by a person seeking to persuade an intelligent audience should be careful. The terms used should be defined and the method of obtaining the statistics should be explained if possible.

* * *

When dealing with a technical topic the persuader must first study the topic so far as it is relevant to the theme to be argued. Then those technical arguments must be reduced to simple concepts that are readily understood by an audience technically uninformed. This often can be achieved by the use of illustration and example.

Economists have some phrases fairly readily understood – for example, 'an over-heated economy'. Care should be taken that this simple phrase is given the same meaning by everyone. A few simple sentences assisted by an example should easily explain what is meant by an 'over-heated economy'. The point is, beware of expressions that may have different meanings to different people. Good examples are 'alcoholic', 'sexual abuse', 'average weekly earnings', 'basic wage', 'cost price index'.

Hopefully, the theme will not be complicated, but the arguments in support may very well be technical and hard to understand. If they are not understood, then they are unlikely to succeed.

On some subjects, for example, stem-cell research or heroin shooting galleries, the audience really needs a brief, informative introduction to the subject before any argument commences. The process of explaining complicated and technical issues will often be time consuming. Eventually one should aim to distil the explanations into a simple proposition that is readily understood and remembered, but is nevertheless accurate.

Like many other aspects of persuasion, simplification is not easy.

Imagine that you are on the board of a manufacturing company and there is a proposal by the managing director to purchase and install a very expensive computer to assist in the manufacturing process. You and your fellow directors have little knowledge of computers, still less of the technicalities involved in computers. The managing director produces a written submission plus a verbal address full of technical propositions that go clean over your head, so you have no idea whether the proposal is a good one or not. As likely as not, you will vote against something you do not understand.

In such a case, the managing director has let you down. He or she should have been able to explain the advantages of the computer and the benefits to the company without putting the directors out of their depths. By all means, technical information could, and perhaps should, have been included in the written proposal, but he or she should have been able to describe the purpose and likely achievements of the computer without recourse to technical jargon.

It is an unfortunate fact that once one has acquired some technical expertise in any specialised field of knowledge there is a temptation to show off one's knowledge at the expense of clarity. Even judgments of the highest courts often spend pages displaying the judicial erudition rather than coming to the point. These people are almost beyond criticism and get away with it, as I suppose do many learned persons at the top of various professions.

These written monuments of learning often achieve little because readers skim through them simply looking for the point of the exercise. It is common these days for busy executives and others to look only at the last few paragraphs of a paper or report.

Since the advent of the internet, it is possible with little effort to pad a report or discourse with a great deal of material, which may well give the impression that the writer or speaker is very learned indeed. I rather doubt whether many people actually read the padding, which is no doubt intended to give an impression of great learning in the author. It also may give the impression of great research by the author.

It might be said that these exercises in vanity do little harm beyond wasting time and perhaps paper. However, they are dangerous in that the time wasted in padding has not been devoted to perfecting the simple propositions that are the crucial part of the exercise leading (one would hope) to the conclusion, which is the whole point of the exercise.

There is a technique, very popular with magistrates and judges, and many other decision makers, of embarking on a long, lengthy judgmental discourse during which no one will be able to guess the result until the very end. I cannot understand why such decisions should not commence 'I find in favour of . . . for the following reasons . . .' If they did, the decisions would probably be much shorter.

Arguments – submissions to an audience, large or small – are not like judgments or decisions. The audience does not have to listen. It can switch off, go to sleep or simply walk out. Only a few of us can address a captive audience. For the rest of us, it is necessary to retain the attention of the audience, and this must be earned. It is necessary for us to make sure the audience understands what we are saying, and, if the topic is complicated, simplification is essential. It is necessary for us to convince the audience, which can only occur if it has understood what we are saying.

If we make our speeches complicated and technical, we may appear learned, before the audience tires of trying to follow what it cannot understand. Some speeches are incomprehensible because the speaker is showing off his or her knowledge and the audience has given up trying to understand. Often, however, the problem is that the speaker has simply forgotten that what he or she knows well may be a mystery to his or her listeners, that what is of intense interest to him or her may be of very little interest to the audience.

The recipient must understand before persuasion can be effected. Therefore, if the subject is complicated, simplification is essential.

By all of this, I do not mean that an audience cannot understand complicated facts, situations or propositions. On the contrary, I believe that a modern audience can do so provided that the trouble is taken to explain, and at the same time the trouble is taken by the speaker to maintain interest. In this process, the complications are simplified, and the audience does understand.

9.

Preparation of a persuasive speech

CAREFUL PREPARATION IS ESSENTIAL to success and the first step is the selection of a theme. In a persuasive speech the theme may seem to provide itself because of the very purpose of the speech, but this is not so. For example, the object of the exercise may be to persuade the audience to vote Labor, Liberal, Green, or Democrat, but of itself this does not provide a theme. The theme will be the reason for so voting or the connecting link between a string of reasons for so voting. From the theme will come the interest, the coherence and the persuasion of the speech. In such a political speech the object is very broad and the possible themes are numerous indeed. Until a suitable theme has been chosen and developed in the mind the embryo speech is a rabble of undeveloped ideas. If a good theme is developed everything else will fall easily into place.

For example, in a speech to save a park from developers, the object is clear; the possible themes are the reasons for preservation. How many reasons should be covered in the speech may be the problem. One might choose the history of the park, which in itself would link up most of the reasons for its preservation. The theme should be chosen for interest and its persuasive effect. For example, koalas in the park would suggest a vibrant theme.

It is very important to estimate the time available for the speech. Sometimes there is a particular time fixed in advance. Some speakers seem to think that they can ignore these fixed times, but not infrequently going over time provokes unnecessary hostility and can undo the effect of an otherwise good speech.

Usually the purpose behind fixed times for speeches is to allow time for other speeches. In such circumstances, going over time shows lack of consideration for others, if not simple selfishness.

The permitted time will be crucial in deciding the theme. If the time is to be short, the theme must permit the speaker to come to the point quickly and probably he or she will deal with one or a few reasons for the cause to be argued.

On the other hand, the time permitted, although fixed, may be quite lengthy, say half an hour, which is quite a long speech in modern times. Many speakers find it quite difficult to keep going for half an hour, but others can go for much longer than that without saying anything useful. In the eighteenth century, parsons spoke for much more than an hour during church services and ushers walked around waking up any sleeping members of the congregation.

An address for half an hour can well be a temptation to try to say much too much and run out of time. It is well to remember that one point well made and driven home is better than a failed effort to make six points.

Some speeches are made with days or weeks or at least hours of preparation. Others are made on the spur of the moment, and are completely impromptu. However, for any speech to succeed there must be a theme, and that theme is not necessarily the immediate purpose or point of the speech. A speech to persuade people to vote for the National Party might have as its theme the depressed state of the dairy industry. A speech to limit hotel hours might have as its theme the evils of alcohol. A speech to prohibit smoking in restaurants might have as its theme the dangers of passive smoking. The theme in a persuasive speech is usually the reason or reasons for being persuaded to accept the purpose or point of the speech.

To prepare a persuasive speech, the first step is to define what you intend to persuade the audience to do or believe. Sometimes clear and precise definition is essential. Many cases of 'waffling' speeches are those where the speaker has not clearly identified the purpose of the speech.

The next step is to think up a theme, usually a reason or collection of reasons why the audience should be persuaded.

In a simple court case, these first two steps should be easy; for example, the accused should be acquitted on the charge of murder (purpose) because he was not there, had no motive and someone else did it (themes). In this case, if the alibi is rock solid, it should be the main theme. The lack of motive can only assist, but saying someone else did it and identifying and naming him could be an unnecessary risk to take. Perhaps the Crown can show conclusively that the suggested murderer could not have done it and the destruction of this reason may well cause the jury to doubt the alibi.

Alibis are very dangerous. Again and again, alibis slip up and juries assume, quite illogically, that a broken alibi signifies a guilty accused.

All of this should be thought out well before counsel rises to address the jury. To simply deliver an unedited rabble of reasons for acquittal is an invitation to disaster.

In the business world, the issue at hand might be whether the manager should be dismissed, and you might have to address the board of directors of the company on this matter. This address will probably be given informally, everybody will be seated, and perhaps there will be several addresses. If you want to save the manager, your object is to persuade others not to dismiss him.

Your themes might be many. He has done nothing wrong, he is a good manager, he cannot easily be replaced, his sacking would cause bad publicity, a pep-talk or reprimand would suffice, and so on. Probably you will have had at least some days' notice of the proposed motion to dismiss the manager. You may well have had informal discussions with fellow directors beforehand.

You should clarify in your own mind what themes you will use, and most importantly which one or more you will stress. Bear in mind that there is no strict time limit for a director's speech at a board meeting, but no one wants it to be too long. You will not do much good for your cause (to save the manager) if you just babble on without editing the material in your mind.

In such a case, it pays to be flexible. Although you may well have a little speech already prepared for the meeting, if you are arguing for the status quo, it may well be wise to listen first to those who want to sack the manager, and fully appreciate their reasons. Of course, if they convince you that they are right, so be it. Persuasion is essentially the most useful form of exchanging ideas.

However, you are not persuaded, but you are now well versed in what arguments have to be refuted or countered to save the manager. You are now in a good position to pick the best arguments to persuade the 'swingers', who have not made up their minds, or even the movers of the motion. By your previous preparation, you already have reasons in your mind for saving the manager.

In this exercise of refutation or counter-argument, preserve the dignity of your opponents. Wherever possible, preserve the essential unity of the board of directors. Remember that one does not lose face if persuaded by reason, or even sentiment, to accept an argument and change one's mind. One loses a great deal of dignity if one is bludgeoned into accepting an argument. It is much easier to persuade gently rather than aggressively.

It should be stressed that a persuader tries to convince the doubters of his or her arguments and even those people completely opposed to them. Some speakers seem to think that humiliation of the enemy is an essential part of the art of persuasion. On the contrary, such humiliation should be avoided whenever possible. One should not think in terms of victory, but rather of exchange of ideas.

To return to the main proposition of this chapter, the preparation of a persuasive speech, the first two steps are to prepare the object and the theme or themes of the speech. This has to be done for any successful persuasive speech.

The next step, as I've explained earlier in the book, is to seek out a good opening.

There are many bad openings available, such as:

'When I was asked to make this speech, I wondered what I was going to talk about.' (Usually such speakers never do find out.)

'I decided before making this speech to look up a good standard dictionary for the meaning of . . .' (This means I am going to be very boring.)

'I really don't know much about this subject but for what it is worth . . .' (This is readily believed.)

'I propose to address you very briefly.' (Such speakers are almost always liars.)

'This is obviously a very dull subject.' (Proof quickly follows.)

All of these openings can be safely discarded, if only because they have been used too often before. If you can think up a good, arresting opening, by all means do so; for example:

'Yesterday as I walked through this park, I saw a koala feeding in the early evening. It was a beautiful, peaceful sight. But in the background I could hear the roar of the developer's bulldozers. How close should he be allowed to come to this previously peaceful place?' (Interesting, vivid and straight to the point.)

'You have all grumbled about this government. Now you have a chance to change it.' (A challenge is always useful in politics.)

'Last week in the Sahara Desert, a child died of starvation in her mother's arms. Does tragedy that far away concern us in prosperous well-fed Australia?' (The plight of a child never fails to get sympathy.)

The idea of each of these openings is to attract attention and to launch into the subject quickly. The worst possible opening describes the speaker's mental searches for ideas (which were never found, as the speech demonstrates).

After the opening comes the statement of the purpose, which may already be clear from the opening but repetition will not hurt. Then, having made the point or purpose of the speech abundantly clear, the themes, the reasons for the purpose, may be developed. Try to think of vivid examples. They live in the audience's mind.

When I was barely in double figures of age, during the Great Depression, the boys of my boarding school (Barker College) were addressed by a visitor about the hard conditions in the world outside. I remember the speaker's words: 'These families cannot afford to buy proper food. What do they eat? Bread and jam.'

All my life I have been haunted by that speech. As a boy, I tried to devise ways and means to solve unemployment. My ideas at eleven or twelve years of age were never implemented but were probably as good or better than the blunders then being made by those in government and commerce.

Another speech I remember from about the same age was the message to Garcia. A soldier in the American war against Spain in 1898 (on the American side, of course) was sent through the enemy line to Garcia with this message which the relator never reveals and in getting to his destination surpassed incredible obstacles by way of the enemy and jungles. But he 'didn't ask why, he didn't ask how – he just did it, said the relator. As I recall it, the soldier risked his life for a useless message (we were at least told that), but that was not the point. Perhaps I remembered this story because it annoyed me. Why risk your life for no purpose? More probably I was stuck by the vivid 'He didn't ask why'.

Of course the English have an even better story of the Crimean War in 1854, when 600 men of the Light Brigade made a ridiculous charge against the Russian artillery, as Tennyson put it, 'Storm'd at with shot and shell, While horse and hero fell'. This was 'not tho' the soldier knew/Some one had blundered.' Ultimately 'Then they rode back but not/Not the six hundred.'

Military disasters provide vivid speech material. Thus Australians have the Anzac legend which is remembered by everyone, but who remembers the Australian victories in France of General Monash in 1918 when he broke the Hindenburg Line?

It can be seen that there is vivid audience grabbing attraction in one of the many stories of a stupid military order followed by a gallant if useless performance by brave soldiers. The great Australian example is the battle of the

Nek at Gallipoli in 1915, when three waves of soldiers were annihilated in a hopeless attack charging against machine guns, the theme of the film *Gallipoli*.

Stories are very often a highly effective means of making a point in a speech. However, as with most things, care has to be taken. It is best for the story to be brief although this may depend on the length of the speech. One should take care lest the speech is taken over by the story and not vice versa.

Speeches vary and all sorts of tactics work – and fail. Beware of delays in coming to the main point. I believe generally in getting there as soon as possible, but speakers vary in this. The obvious risk of delay in coming to the point is that the main point may well be missed altogether, or at least obscured.

Some experienced speakers prepare all that I have mentioned so far in their heads and make the speech without ever having made any notes. Such an approach is flexible and often leads to great audience contact, but it is difficult to do and usually can only be done after years of plentiful experience. This method carries the risk that a good point will be forgotten. I have made many speeches this way, but I must confess that almost invariably I remember after the speech a good idea that I forgot to include. However, the audience never knows.

It is probably better to jot down some headings on a piece of paper. If one numbers the headings, say one to five, one can remember when making the speech if all the headings have been covered without actually producing the paper in front of the audience. Thus one can get all the advantages of appearing to be as competent as the speaker who never makes a note, but not take as many risks.

Many speakers make very extensive notes, which they use as an aide-mémoire when making the speech. For some speakers this is necessary. A very big thick bundle of notes is often plonked on the lectern by a speaker who commences with 'I shall only be brief'.

It probably does put off an audience if bulky notes are used. Some speakers, however, doubt their memories to make a quotation and have it all written out. That is understandable, but if the speaker has devised some original phrase or sentence that might have a striking effect, all is spoiled if it is read from copious notes.

Good speakers like to speak with minimal notes in order to maintain audience contact. Furthermore, the speech preparation is usually not too rigid so that the speaker can work through one aspect of his or her speech that appears to be getting a friendly reception and perhaps rephrase another aspect where the audience reaction is not so favourable. Particularly in a persuasive speech, audience reaction is crucial to a good speaker. Over the years, he or she develops an instinct to discern the difference between polite attention and agreement, even enthusiastic agreement. Such a speaker can see when the audience has lost the plot or disagrees, and attempts are then made to win over or win back that audience.

One can probably compare a good speaker with a helmsman of a surf-boat guiding it through the waves, and never taking his eyes off the waves.

Frequently barristers address a judge or a jury for lengthy periods, sometimes days. If the only audience is the judge, there will usually be a lot of express audience reaction. When there is such reaction, it is foolish to press on with a carefully prepared speech. That reaction, by way of judicial comment, must be dealt with immediately, and the prepared speech must be suspended, or even at times abandoned, at least in part.

Careful arguments are often prepared by barristers for appellate courts consisting of three or five judges. These arguments are usually preceded by written submissions so that at least the outline of the argument is already well understood by the court. Thereafter, counsel's argument may be an enlargement or development of the written submissions, but it will also be an answer to numerous questions or comments from the bench. Since appellate judges may well disagree between themselves, questions and comments must be answered carefully, even if they have to be answered immediately. Successful appellate advocacy depends on extensive study of the subject and a flexible approach so as to persuade people who often express their views forcibly.

This type of ordeal is not confined to appellate counsel. Non-lawyers often have to put submissions before councils or company boards who can be just as difficult as appellate judges. The submission in such a case is often preceded by a written submission and the persuader is again confronted by comments and questions, some of which may be very difficult to answer.

When arguing before such courts, committees or boards, there are a few good rules for preparation:

1. Do your best to know backwards the limited subject in question. Be prepared for a possible expansion of the subject.
2. When confronted with aggressive behaviour, one must not lose one's way or one's temper. Therefore the preparation must centre on a clear objective towards which the persuader will continue to move despite all opposition.
3. Try to devise an interesting, even an entertaining, way to put the argument. A joke can sometimes ease the way. Nobody likes to listen to a boring argument.

Preparation for this type of argument well illustrates the words adapted from Bobbie Burns' poem 'To a Mouse':

> The best laid plans of mice and men
> Gang aft awry.

It is rare for such an address to go according to plan. It is best to have a flexible plan, perhaps alternative plans, but the purpose of the address must remain unchanged and inflexible. In some circumstances, however, the purpose may become a lost cause, but an alternative that is better than defeat is available. That possibility should be part of the preparation so that it does not come as a complete surprise.

Addressing a bench of judges or a committee is difficult indeed. The preparation has to be very extensive so as to cover all possible attitudes from those to be persuaded. Even with such preparation, someone may come up with a new and unforeseen concept that may destroy most of the preparatory work. One can but do one's best.

Addressing a jury, on the other hand, one will receive no express reaction or comment. You will be asked no awkward questions. There was one incident when a leading Queen's Counsel was in full flight and a juror said, 'That's not the evidence.' Counsel had a transcript. In those days, the jury rarely took notes and as today did not have a transcript. But the juror was right. Never underestimate a jury. Such an event, however, is very rare.

The jury might be addressed for an hour, hours or sometimes for days in a long case. In many cases today the jury will take notes, and the note-taking may give some clue to counsel as to how the address is being received.

Note-taking observation by counsel is guesswork.

I have seen some jurors writing at what seemed to me important places in the evidence or address, but who knows what the note said? (Today by law, any inquiry as to the notes after the case would be a criminal offence. The jury's deliberations are supposed to be forever secret.) So, as you confidently hammer home a point, the juror may be writing a note in your favour or a complete rebuttal. You may guess but you rarely know.

Preparation for a jury address usually seeks to ensure that no crucial or even mildly important point in favour of your client is omitted. Therefore it is wise to have a check-list of all points to be made and this will be checked before you sit down. However, this exhaustive approach may be counterproductive. It is better to seek one's best points rather than all one's points, as I shall discuss later.

For such an address, the same outline applies as for other speeches: opening, purpose clearly defined (this is usually obvious), themes developed, conclusion.

It would be rare for such an address to be made without preparatory notes. There should at least be a check list of points to be made. The notes of preparation, which might well be extensive, should not amount to a dreary paper to be read to a bored jury. Eye contact and audience observation is absolutely essential in an address to a jury – in fact, to any audience.

The same applies to any address to a committee, council, company board or other small body of persons whom you hope to persuade. Preparation should ensure that you do not miss any important matter. The notes should permit you to be flexible and maintain eye contact.

For all speeches, time should be considered. Courts like to keep their lists intact by not going over a time allotted for a case. Committees and boards are most anxious to get through heavy agendas and do not want your particular cause to leave many other matters unattended and unresolved. Quite frequently, councils and boards set fixed times for submissions. One is not told in advance what that time will be, although common sense should tell you that you will have to be quick and to the point.

On one occasion, I addressed a council on behalf of a ratepayer. I was told just before I started that I had one minute and no more. Before coming, I knew precisely what my client wanted and I had discovered one excellent reason why he should succeed in the submission. It was, in fact, quite easy to make the submission briefly and effectively but I confess to being surprised when I was told by the chairman that my speech had taken exactly one minute. I had not looked at my watch. The submission succeeded, much to my client's delight.

Where a fixed time for speaking is set well in advance, some speakers actually rehearse the speech. I never did. A speech will never come out in quite the same words and in the same time when it is delivered twice. Furthermore, a speech delivered for the second time tends to be stale and artificial. Rather, one must prepare the outlines and detail of the speech, distinguishing what must be said, what ought to be said and what might well be said. What might well be said may, if necessary, be deleted when the speech is delivered. It is material in reserve.

I should stress again that when one is speaking at a conference where there is a list of speakers, it is selfish to go over time and intrude on the next speaker's time.

Perhaps it is necessary for me to say that there are exceptions to just about every rule or guide in public speaking. Some people compose a speech and then rehearse it like a play, and succeed. Winston Churchill's speeches were very carefully prepared, word by word and, I believe, rehearsed.

Some people rise to the occasion on the spur of the moment, inspired by the circumstances, and make splendid speeches that are composed as they go along. These are usually experienced speakers, but, sometimes when a cause is deeply felt, such speeches are made well by inexperienced speakers.

There is no doubt that if you feel deeply about a topic, you have the basis of a good speech, provided that you appreciate that others may have very different views, and you take those views into account. It is still necessary to pay regard to what I have described as the outlines of a good speech.

I now come to the speech that is written out in its entirety. A typical example is a principal's speech on a school's speech day, which is often printed in full in the program. A wise principal will not read this out but rather make a much shorter speech referring to extracts perhaps.

Some didactic organisations require the speaker to write a paper before the meeting that is later printed and purports to be the precise words of the speech actually delivered. In some cases that is true and the audience listens to a lengthy speech read out and later printed and published. The reading is often a boring business.

Learned papers are often persuasive but go through the same publishing procedure. Such a paper may well have more than one object and many themes. It may well be hard to follow when delivered, but it is hoped it will be read again by the audience, usually some time later. The advantages are the preservation of the learning contained in the speech and perhaps a more careful expression of complicated concepts. The disadvantages are all in the delivery, which can be deadly dull and hard, if not impossible, to follow.

Such a speech should still have the essential outline of opening, object, themes (reasons) and conclusion. It would be wise to include interesting, even amusing, examples to retain the audience's attention. The audience for such speeches, however, is usually learned or anxious to learn, and substantially different from an ordinary audience.

Finally there is the speaker who must write out the speech word for word as it is to be delivered. Again, such a speech should have the essential outline I have described. It may be the address of a tyro scared that stage fright would make any other type of speech impossible. It may be the speech of a great speaker, an Abraham Lincoln or a Winston Churchill. In both cases, the preparation is the same. It is usual for this type of speech to be prepared over a long period. In the case of the great speeches so prepared, large slabs (or the whole) were learned off by heart as part of the preparation. Sometimes the speech was delivered to a trial audience, or even a mirror, so that the speaker could practise the inflections and pauses so as to try the effect.

These great speeches, written in full and recited rather than delivered, are in a class of their own. The speaker prepares a script for himself, which he or she later delivers as an actor believing in the script.

I fear that these days many speeches by politicians and others are written by speechwriters. It is said (hopefully) that the speaker checks and adds to the prepared script, which he or she delivers as his or her own words. It is a modern development and in my opinion it is not a good one. For me, the idea of reading or reciting someone else's words as my own is rather dishonest. Yet I suppose I do not object to a speaker getting assistance and ideas from others. The difficult question may be when are the words so much those of someone else that the speaker is sailing under false colours?

If a student gets a bright person to impersonate him or her in an examination, that is obviously dishonest cheating. If a politician recites the words of another as his own, what is that?

It might be said that we should know that politicians get someone else to write their speeches, but do we? Only some speeches are ghost-written. How do we know which ones? We vote for Joe Bloggs because of his sincere advanced thinking as evidenced in speeches, which we do not know were written by his ghost-writer.

No doubt some company directors do the same. No Trade Practices Act prohibition appears to encompass ghost-writing. A student who fails in a university thesis to acknowledge quotations from other sources, and claims them as his or her own, is guilty of plagiarism, a serious academic offence. But it is not the same if a cabinet minister does so. Why?

Only some forms of dishonesty are illegal, it would appear.

Finally I should refer to a not unknown phenomenon. Some speakers prepare two speeches and decide which one to use after assessing the audience. Usually the preparation includes an opening sentence or paragraph common to both speeches. The audience reaction to that brief passage will determine which speech will then be delivered.

Often the two prepared speeches will be quite similar and sometimes it is really only one speech with variable parts. For a persuasive speech to an unknown audience, a flexibility in preparation that will permit the speaker to adapt his or her arguments to those who hear them has obvious advantages.

As a matter of interest, this technique of preparing two speeches is not so uncommon when the speaker proposes to be funny, particularly in an after-dinner speech. Funny speeches are always risky. Sometimes, for reasons that are not obvious, excellent jokes fall flat and the speaker is left non-plussed. If the would-be humorist presses on with more jokes, the result is likely to be a quite pathetic humiliation of the speaker. However, if he or she sees the opening jokes fall flat, if he or she has prepared two speeches, he or she can abandon the first, and take up the second, pretending that there never was any intention to be funny.

(Many years ago, when I was very young, I tried university-style humour on a Rostrum audience of businessmen. It was a disaster, and I did not have an alternative speech.)

I recommend this precaution to those whom W.S. Gilbert called (in 'The Mikado') 'All comic fellows, funny men and clowns of private life'.

The key to a successful speech is a clear purpose in the speech, clearly introduced, skilfully propounded and effectively concluded. In preparation, as I have said before and can hardly repeat too often, you must ask yourself the two crucial questions: what am I trying to achieve, and why should this audience listen.

10.

The delivery of a speech

IN MY INTRODUCTION TO this book, I included a method of improving voice production by breathing into the chest and then speaking out from the chest. With very little practice, this can vastly improve the volume and depth of a speaker's voice.

Even if gifted with a good voice, be careful about rejecting an offered microphone. The fact that there is a microphone may well indicate that there are difficulties with the acoustics. With experience, a speaker will have a fairly accurate idea as to how far his or her voice will carry, but it is wise to remember that some rooms are tricky and deceptive in terms of acoustics, especially for after-dinner speeches when there may well be a lot of background noise.

If you are to use a microphone, try to test it first. Especially try to ascertain how close your mouth should be to the speaker on that particular microphone as microphones vary.

Without a microphone, voice volume is important. If one learns the art of first breathing in and then speaking out through the mouth with the expulsion of air, you will soon learn how not only to enlarge but to regulate the volume of your voice. Once you are confident that your voice can easily be heard at the back of the room, you can then fairly easily regulate how loud you should be, so as to minimise strain on yourself and achieve a comfortable volume.

Sometimes with an after-dinner speech, you may find a clatter as some people continue eating. It is probably best to pause if there is such a noise rather than try to speak over it. The sudden silence will usually terrify the would-be eater and the interruption will cease. Trying to shout over the noise is not as effective as pausing.

If the speech is suddenly drowned by an aircraft overhead or by thunder, pause till the noise eases. If, while pausing, you can think up a witty or pleasant remark for the resumption of your speech, you will achieve excellent audience contact.

In most situations it is best to avoid shouting. Remember that shouting can play tricks with your voice and produce a quite unpleasant result. Several times I have seen a good speaker work himself (the shouters are usually men) up to a frenzy when he started to shout. Suddenly the audience laughed. Sometimes a funny interjection followed. In a flash a good speech was ruined. Shouting tends to indicate loss of self-control.

The next consideration is speed. The usual error in speech delivery is speaking too fast. It is a very common practice for speakers to speak far too quickly in order to say everything they want to say in the available time. The worst example of this is the speaker with a speech entirely written out that is far too long. An attempt is made to complete a speech made for twice the available time by racing against the clock. Literally nothing registers and the audience endures a frustrating ordeal.

Often the reason for speaking too fast is simply nervousness, but speaking too fast simply aggravates the situation. Careful pauses tend to calm the nerves and increase confidence.

It is important to appreciate that the speed of a speech is a most important ingredient. A good speaker pauses to achieve effect, or to let the audience comprehend and digest what has been said. Then the speaker may speed up to achieve urgency before another dramatic pause, and so on. Speed is very important when telling a story.

Charles Dickens gave marvellous performances reading his own novels to very large audiences. The tone of his voice, the speed of his delivery, and its intensity matched the narrative so as to achieve a tremendously dramatic effect. One notable example was his reading of the death of Nancy in *Oliver Twist*. He described her murder and her murderer Bill Sykes' flight with a dramatic intensity that profoundly moved the audience. The strain of such reading undermined his health and was probably responsible for his early death. Perhaps it is just as well that few of us can achieve such dramatic effects in a speech, but Charles Dickens illustrated the power of the voice when the words of the speech are powerful. The voice varies its volume, its intensity, its tone and its speed to reflect the language used.

Do not try to slavishly copy a good speaker who achieves such results. Rather try and understand how he or she does it and try and adapt the same methods to suit your voice and your personality. Only a great deal of practice will achieve dramatic results, but if you try to develop your own personality and speak naturally, even conversationally, albeit to a large audience, the variation of speed, tone, volume and intensity will come naturally.

It is a great asset to have a good voice – clear, pleasant, expressive and powerful – but it is not essential. Perhaps the most moving and therefore the most effective speech I ever heard was a sermon delivered many years ago by a visiting parson to St Andrew's Anglican Church,

Roseville, when I was a very young man. The preacher began by apologising for his voice, which he described as a handicap that he could not help. It was indeed a dreadful voice, gravelly and most unpleasant, with little ability to vary its tones. But as he proceeded he developed an intensity and sincerity that was quite overwhelming. This message and the language of his message transcended the handicap of his voice. He appeared to be, and probably was, inspired. The congregation hung on his every word, and he concentrated on a single simple but important message. I can still remember that message, even though I may have doubted whether he was right. However, by and large, he convinced me.

The real test of a good speech is its ultimate impact. If that impact lasts a lifetime, then the speech was indeed outstanding.

Previously I considered the great differences between listening to a speech and reading a document. In particular, the listener cannot go back over the speech as can the reader. If the point is missed and not repeated, it is lost forever. If the point lost is the key to the whole speech, then the speech is wasted. Accordingly, pause is one of the most important aspects of speech delivery.

Pause can serve to emphasise and lend drama. Even more importantly, pause gives the thoughts of the audience time to catch up with the thoughts of the speaker.

The length of a pause is obviously dependent upon the intention of the speaker. Dramatic pause can be quite lengthy so as to achieve audience impact. Pause for laughter should permit the audience to enjoy the joke before the speech continues. A pause to permit the audience to absorb and understand the sentence may be quite short or quite long. (In a rowdy meeting, with a hostile audience, pause has its dangers, as I shall describe when dealing with interjections in the next chapter.)

Gesture is difficult for some if not most speakers. It is dangerous to try to copy someone else who has good gesture; it will look hopelessly artificial.

Gesture eventually comes naturally to most speakers, although in some not so common cases it never comes at all. If that is so with you, do not worry. Some excellent speeches are made by speakers who do not gesture at all. In fact, it is much better to have no gesture than some artificial movement of the hands and arms that is simply distracting.

Telling a story during a speech often encourages gesture natural to the particular speaker. Many people gesture in ordinary conversation. Others remain quite rigid. It is an advantage to gesture during a speech, but a good speech can be made without gesture.

Stance is sometimes a problem. Some speakers stand still, particularly behind a lectern. Others wander over a stage. A wandering speaker needs to pay heed to whether his physical meanderings are distracting the audience's attention from what he or she is saying. It may well be so.

Standing up straight is often advocated, but one should be relaxed. The best course is to be comfortable but avoid distracting slouches or other mannerisms.

Gesture and stance are very personal to the speaker. The essential aim is for the speaker to be comfortable and at ease, and at the same time not distracting the audience from the message of his or her speech, or annoying the audience by his or her appearance.

If gesture is mechanical and artificial, far from aiding the speaker, it is a handicap. If wandering around distracts or annoys the audience, it is also a handicap. If the speaker has no gesture and a rigid stance, it might be well for that stance to loosen a little. The Buckingham Palace sentry stance is, in itself, distracting.

There is also the speaker's appearance to consider. Appearing in beach attire before a formally dressed meeting might offend quite a few members of the audience, and this type of offence is quite unnecessary. Obviously a handsome speaker has an asset to impress the audience but an ordinary speaker will not suffer from appearing reasonably neat and tidy. The speaker's dress should try to match that of the audience.

Some of these matters might be considered relatively unimportant but all unnecessary handicaps should be avoided. Sometimes one of these minor matters can be quite important to some members of the audience.

The speaker's time of arrival is another matter that is important to the audience. It is most undesirable for the speaker to be late. The meeting is annoyed and the speaker may well be flustered and embarrassed at the commencement of the speech. The speaker should try to arrive early, not late. If the speaker is late, there should be an apology. Usually the apology is readily accepted, but a failure to apologise is often resented.

Although it is very true that 'to err is human', it is distracting and annoying if a speech contains a liberal serving of 'ers' while the speaker thinks. It is surprising how many experienced speakers continually say 'er'. It has become a habit. Sometimes it seems to be a mark of the speaker's self-importance, and is resented by the audience. Many practised speakers, especially parliamentarians, 'er' in a condescending way, as though they are doing this audience a favour by addressing it. Others give the impression that their 'ers' are the necessary expressions of their magnificent brains. 'Ers' are annoying, distracting and unnecessary. All speakers are inclined to 'er'. Good speakers try to control that inclination.

'Ers' in a speech should be eliminated by practice and willpower. Do not permit them to become a bad habit. Often the habit continues and grows worse over the years.

Once a determined effort is made to correct it, the habit usually disappears, but it can return.

Copious notes on a lectern usually evoke no real problems. If there is a lectern provided, notes are probably expected. However, voluminous wads of notes at weddings and social occasions provoke well-based forebodings in the audience of a long, boring speech. A committee or council with a long agenda will feel an immediate and natural hostility towards a speaker with a thick wad of notes.

Just as your arguments should be, so far as you can make them, acceptable to your audience, so should your appearance, gesture and mannerisms. Therefore, if you have to use notes, use compressed headings, if possible on a card or only one or two sheets of paper.

If you hope to persuade an audience, you must try to avoid distracting or annoying it. I have been amazed in recent years how young counsel will be late to court, how speakers arrive late and the meeting has to wait and there is not even an apology. When you are late, you are telling the court or the meeting that you regard your time as more important than its time. What a way to start! What an unnecessary handicap to give yourself!

How risqué or obscene can be the language of a speaker? Can he or she use swear words? These days, few words have not been frequently heard by the most refined of us, but there are some words that still sound quite shocking in most meetings. The use of such words to get audience attention, or for emphasis, or to get a laugh, is riskier than some speakers believe. When obscene words are used, most people today do not protest, lest they be regarded as old fogies, but that does not stop them feeling hostile to the speaker. Swear words should only be used with care, and not as a matter of course. The whole idea of a swear word is emphasis. If every sentence contains swear words then they serve no useful purpose and are merely annoying.

Although today we are gender equal, many women do not like swear words, and there are some which they intensely dislike. When those words are used they pretend not to be offended, but in fact they may strongly resent the speaker's use of obscene language. In this regard the older the audience the greater the risk when using swear words.

A good speaker watches the audience, even a large audience. Martin Luther King, even if speaking into a microphone to a large audience, still seemed to look at everyone. In smaller meetings, eye contact can be very effective.

One needs to be careful not to pick one person who is the sole recipient of your eye contact. This can be embarrassing to that person and annoying to everyone else. Your eyes should wander over and encompass the whole audience so as to give each individual the impression that the speech is directed at him or her.

At the same time as you watch the audience, you can assess its reaction. It may need waking up by a loud voice or a dramatic statement. It may be intrigued. It can often express silent opposition. Sometimes the opposition will be not so silent.

Especially if you are on a time limit, but in any event, it is good to be able to place your watch where you can glance at it without being observed doing so. If this is not possible, the glance at one's wristwatch should be quick and non-distracting. It is normally essential to keep your eye firmly on the time.

It is obviously desirable to make as direct a speech as possible to the audience. If notes are used, they should be unobtrusive and only be there for the occasional glance. To stop dead while you read your notes is to sever audience contact and give an impression of incompetence.

However, if the speech is an entirely pre-written paper, a direct address is impossible. It should not be necessary to read every word, still less give the speech word for word. If you wrote the paper yourself, you should have a good memory of it. Therefore you should be able to deliver most of it from memory in similar but not identical words, adding, subtracting and ad-libbing. If perchance you depart from the script to such an extent as to miss some of it, anyone interested can read it later. If time does not permit the whole paper to be read, part will have to be omitted. On no account should you try to beat the clock by reading faster and faster. That is futile and foolish.

What do you do if you suddenly, while on your feet, strike a blank? This can happen to young as well as elderly speakers. The mind loses the thread and there you are on your feet not quite knowing where you are or what to say next. This is a rare event but it can happen to anyone. Normally it is momentary and probably only the speaker will know it has happened. The best remedy is to think back rather than forward, repeat what you have just said, and with luck you will jump the barriers at the second attempt. It could be likened to an old car going over a hill on the second try. You do not press the accelerator and simply stall the engine; you fall back and try again.

Do not panic if it is a very bad gap in the mind. I have known a good speaker to say 'Wait a moment, I have lost myself', or some such words. The audience was sympathetic, the mental gap passed, and on the speaker went.

Such occurrences are very rare but can be frightening.

Other accidents can happen while you are speaking, such as papers fluttering to the ground and glasses of water falling. Many speakers like to keep a glass of water handy, particularly for long speeches. Keep it away from where your gesturing arms might hit it. It can be a messy and inconvenient accident. Avoid placing it near papers or books that you may reach for during the speech. If you do go in for wide-flung gestures, stand clear of the table or lectern where the water may be.

While I was still an articled clerk, I was in court when a barrister nicknamed 'Drinkwater' was appearing. The solicitor with me told me to watch for him spilling the water. Sure enough, Drinkwater had a great thirst and was constantly pouring himself more and more water. He was a natural fiddler with his books and papers, and again and again the glass of water was imperilled but nevertheless stood firm. Then, just as one thought nothing was going to happen, a wild gesture sent the glass flying. This was no mere spill but a great splash drenching not only Drinkwater's brief and papers, but most of the bar table.

Then followed his mopping-up efforts, which were as incompetent as his previous carryings-on. I doubt whether anyone, including the judge, heard anything he had said. He was well known and everyone was watching in anticipation.

I saw him several times in other cases. He never failed his audience.

In some halls one is interrupted by aircraft passing overhead or other loud noises. I have had to stop addressing a court because of a storm. If the break is likely to be substantial, make a mental or written note of where you were when interrupted. Try to pretend that the interruption did not matter and the audience will so regard it.

Normally an audience is sympathetic to the speaker on such occasions.

I have said a lot about speakers who have too much to say and make the mistakes of speaking too fast and going over time. Probably there are more speakers who run out of ideas before their time expires. If this happens, the wise course is to wind up and conclude. The foolish course is to try to pad out the remaining time. If you have nothing more to say, you should stop. There is no disgrace in concluding before time runs out.

With a hostile or difficult audience, it is important to keep your temper. Whatever happens, a speaker should continue to be polite and friendly. It is possible, however, to attack an audience and thereby effectively impart a message. This used to be a common practice of preachers starting with John the Baptist who succeeded many Hebrew prophets and was followed by many modern preachers such as Billy Graham. Hellfire preaching is not so common today, whereas in the beginning of the twentieth century there were preachers who, in my father's words, 'made you feel the heat of the flames'. Nevertheless, the modern preacher may draw attention in no uncertain terms to the sins or shortcomings of the congregation. If you go to church you should expect this from time to time.

Outside of church we may be made aware of our failures to support charities, to drink moderately, to drive carefully and unselfishly, to be fair and honest in business and so on, but the non-clerical speaker is wise to do these things tactfully and not by thundering condemnation.

Sometimes an audience responds very enthusiastically to a speech. So encouraged, a speaker can get carried away. Perhaps the result of that will be foolish extreme statements by the speaker, and that is the subject of the next chapter.

All that I have said about delivery of a speech is important, but these matters are subsidiary to the essential elements of a good speech, namely purpose and themes. There are too many speeches today which are well delivered but in fact the speaker has nothing worthwhile to say.

11.

The extreme statement, provocation and interjections

ONE OF THE PERILS of controversy is the extreme statement. One word leads to another. One statement leads to another. Annoyance takes control of reason. In no time, you find yourself defending or extolling an extreme position in which you do not believe. You have been stung by the other person's statements into taking up an extreme and probably indefensible position. You can get into the same position if carried away by support from the audience.

No one likes to admit to being wrong. So in no time you are saying things that you do not believe. It is strange how easy it is to get into this ridiculous position.

For example, there may have been an industrial strike

by a trade union. You think this strike is unjustified. You may well be right. Then you get into an argument about it, and, to your surprise, you wake up to the fact that you have been arguing that all trade unions are communist, or all Australian workers are lazy, or some other ridiculous proposition.

Setting it out baldly, as I have just done, you may think it unlikely that your tongue could run away with you like that. However, it is surprising how easy it is for this to happen.

Anyone who has been a member of a political party and attended local branch meetings will have heard many extreme statements, whether from the right or left. There appears to be an idea around that the more extreme statements you make, the better party member you are.

In big public party conventions, the delegates often, but not invariably, realise that care needs to be taken with statements that might be reported in the media. In little party branch meetings, the faithful can let their hair down and let off steam. So it is that Liberal and Labor supporters tend to describe their opponents as though they are members of a criminal conspiracy. Perhaps it is all good clean fun. The members at the meeting often laugh about it later. In fact, party members tend to be quite good friends with those of the opposite party whom they meet on polling booths, as I mentioned previously.

Of course, sometimes wild talk leads to wild action, such as the New Guard in the early 1930s when ordinary, respectable, middle-class people armed and drilled and prepared to take over the government during the grim days of the Depression and the government of J.T. Lang. It never pays to lose one's sense of proportion, or to be carried away by the romance of extreme measures. Fortunately the New Guard came to nothing other than De Groote cutting the ribbon when the Harbour Bridge opened in 1932. I do not approve of wild, foolish political ranting that some people may take seriously. Obviously it is wise counsel to be careful of what you say on all occasions, but few of us follow this advice. It is a fact of life that all of us tend to say things that we do not really mean.

This is an unfortunate feature of many family lives and it can lead to divorce. It may cause resentment, hatred, assaults and even murder. One word leads to another, especially if the words are angry words.

Probably the main cause of extreme, foolish statements is loss of temper.

Some people argue offensively so as to get under your skin. That type of argument convinces or converts nobody, but in political and other fields it can be useful. Your opponent is lured into extreme statements from which he or she finds it difficult to retreat. Such tactics are hardly ethical, but they are often employed.

In my practice at the bar, I occasionally came across an opponent whose technique was deliberate provocation. Such people are met in politics and in all walks of life where persuasion is practised. There are other people whose conduct is unintentionally provocative, and who achieve the same results, whether intended or not.

The advantage of provocation, of getting under your opponent's skin, is to throw him or her off balance. I have seen this done mercilessly in court. I have had it done to me.

In the early 1950s, car-hire companies were not nearly as popular and as well patronised as they are today. Some had a bad reputation for hiring out faulty cars, not like the near new cars hired today. I appeared for a hire company whose car had been damaged by a customer and we were suing for the cost of repairs.

It was a trivial case between insignificant parties before the not-so-important District Court. Yet by one of those strange quirks that one finds in the law, the customer had powerful friends who came to his aid when he was furious with my client the hire company. To my dismay, as a very junior counsel in a fairly minor court, I found myself up against one of Sydney's leading Queen's Counsel before a weak judge who gave my opponent full licence to do what he wanted. In no time I was bullied, provoked and crushed, not once but many times. In no time I was completely off balance, struggling to survive. Of course I lost, but whether I should have lost is doubtful.

That is one case that I shall never forget, a trivial case where the defeat was only a minor annoyance to my client, but a devastating humiliation for myself. I can well remember struggling to maintain my equilibrium and failing dismally. Everything I said or did seemed to go wrong.

I bore no resentment against that Queen's Counsel. It was one of those things.

One can argue about the ethics of deliberate provocation. There can be little doubt about how effective it can be. The idea is to produce loss of balance and loss of judgment in your opponent, and in this context one's opponent may well make statements that may be bitterly regretted later.

On the other hand, many people in arguments drift into the perils of extremity without much help from their opponents. It is just part of human nature.

The earlier one retreats from absurdity, the better. Failure to retreat leads to giving a false and self-derogatory expression of one's opinions. If you find yourself in this silly position, the best course is to retreat, as quickly as possible.

Better still, do not get into such a position. The secret is calm self-control in an argument. This is surprisingly difficult. We all have our tender spots and some arguers are very skilful in probing these sensitive areas, often deliberately.

It is all part of the basic rule of argument: never, never lose control of what you are saying. This is easily said but it is not easy to do.

Many arguers sneer, and sneering is hard to take. But this is the time when it is most important to retain full self-control. It is easier to do this once you appreciate that apparent indifference to sneers and insults is as annoying to the sneerer as his sneers are to you. If you just remain calm, the crisis will pass and you will not say something foolish.

In political circles and parliaments, arguments are often conducted not to persuade, but to condemn and belittle. This is particularly so around question time as broadcast and telecast. Apparently it is felt that voters like nasty, sneering politicians. I suppose the idea is that if you despise the opposition you will vote for the government, or vice versa. Perhaps their philosophy is no matter how bad we are they are worse.

Of course, even outside politics, wild enthusiasm by the audience for a cause can easily provoke the speaker into making foolish and extreme statements. Probably in the sphere of protection of the environment there are some of the best examples of extreme statements. The 'greenies', the environmentalists, seem to work themselves up into a frenzy with an ease only matched by their opponents doing the same thing. For example, in the Tasmanian forest disputes, wild, extreme statements abound from both sides. Each side attacks and provokes the other, intensifying the dispute and well concealing the merits of the argument.

The intensity of the feeling for the forests is matched by the intensity of feeling on the part of those whose livelihoods are at stake. Hence, arguments are bitter, language is extreme, and worthwhile compromise is difficult to achieve.

In a democracy, there are so many causes being pursued, and there is so much news. Anyone advocating a particular cause struggles to be heard and gain attention. The obvious way to get this attention is to make extreme statements and perform extreme acts, such as chaining oneself to a tree. Thus, by the time public attention is achieved, the opposing parties tend to be tied to extreme positions that prevent compromise or even reasonable discussion.

This is a serious problem of our democracy and the media. Reasonable argument, gentle persuasion, is not news. Arrogant rudeness, provocation, wild extreme statements and actions are news, and those who want to advance causes want to *be* news.

Do these extreme methods achieve results or do they merely stir up unnecessary opposition?

I was a counsel frequently acting for the causes of law and order during the Vietnam War demonstrations.

They were stirring days; there were street demonstrations, processions, court demonstrations, insults to magistrates, even on one occasion a storming of the court. Looking back now, it is surprising indeed how little sensible reasonable discussion there was about the merits of the intervention in Vietnam. Even today, protagonists argue as if there never was a case for the other side.

There is a great deal of similarity between the Vietnam situation and the Iraq situation. Discussion is still in extreme terms and the opposition of whatever point of view is insulted, belittled and derided. Yet again I wonder whether anything much is achieved by the extreme argument that is invariably matched by extremity on the other side.

There is a great deal to be said for reasonable debate, gentle persuasion and correct conclusions. Such conclusions will not be achieved by mere agitation and provocation, newsworthy as such matters may be.

From all of this, I seek to demonstrate both the power and the futility of extreme statements. At such times of extremity, gentle persuasion may be a voice crying out in the wilderness.

Talleyrand, Napoleon's Minister for Foreign Affairs, once said: 'In times of crisis, the greatest danger is the enthusiasm of inexperienced persons.' Add to that the luring intoxication of the modern media and it can be easily understood why we seem to lurch from blunder to blunder.

How, then, is the gentle persuader to handle all of this? Whether intended or not, the result of provocation is likely to be to throw the opponent off balance. The answer is obvious, namely to keep one's temper and stay firm and unruffled. Of course, this is much easier said than done.

It does not pay to be too sensitive. By and large, the only person who takes much notice of a personal attack on yourself is yourself. Others are more concerned about their own affairs. If you do not take much notice yourself, the attack fails.

Not infrequently, people came to me wanting to sue a newspaper for some comment when their names appeared in print. When one's own name appears in print it stands out like a beacon, but only to you. Others may give it a quick glance and move up to the sporting page, the share prices, or whatever. The effect on others of an article containing your name is often so insignificant that even if the article may be defamatory, it is hardly worth the risks of suing.

So it is with personal insults and slighting remarks. Reacting to them is often much worse than ignoring them.

An obvious reaction to provocation is counter-provocation. An insult may provoke a much more effective insult. After all, one is entitled to the right of self-defence.

The decision to retaliate or ignore usually has to be made quickly. Effective retaliation is very satisfying. However, it may divert you from the effective advancement of your cause, and, despite your retaliation, you may still be thrown off balance.

You are only human and you can hardly be expected not to retaliate. You do not want to be a wimp. You must, however, appreciate the dangers of retaliation.

You do not want to come down to the same level as your provoker. If the attack on you involves coarse, shouted, or even obscene language, there is no need to shout back in kind. How much more effective is the quiet, polite but devastating reply?

Such a reaction also helps you to maintain your balance and not lose your temper. You must never lose your temper. You may pretend to be enraged, but you must never lose self-control.

Provocation is by no means always loud and obvious. It is more deadly if it is subtle, and perhaps only understood by you. This subtle provocation is best ignored, especially if only you understood it.

A difficult situation arises when you are making a speech and you suffer interjections from the audience. Interjections comprise two serious dangers for the speaker. The train of thought and the effect of the speech may be lost, but, more seriously, the speaker may be stung into a foolish reply.

If you have a quick wit, it is often possible to give a good reply to an interjection as, for example, did the famous politician George Reid, often called two-faced because he changed his mind about the need for federation of the Australian states.

'You're two-faced, George,' called the interjector.

'Who said that?' said George. (This is a favourite tactic of good speakers who thus gain time to think up a reply.)

'I said that,' said the interjector, standing up.

'I can see you're not two-faced,' said George, 'otherwise you would have left that face at home.'

The audience laughed, loved George for his wit, and on he went.

Robert Menzies was famous for his replies to interjectors. People came in crowds to his meetings mainly to hear him tilting with the interjectors. But he could get carried away as he did once when election-campaigning in Tasmania. Stung by a chorus of interjections, he exploded, saying words to the effect 'I didn't come down here to address the descendants of the convicts.'

That was many years ago when a lot of people were sensitive about having a convict ancestor. The remark was widely published and did Menzies a lot of harm in that election. The hostile interjectors had achieved their purpose.

If you do not have a quick wit, it is best to ignore the interjection, or join in the laughter, and thus be regarded as a good sport.

If you are able to make the quick effective reply, do so. But be careful.

If you are having a bad time with interjections, one useful way forward is to tell a story. If it is a good story, the audience will want to hear it, and often will themselves silence the interjector.

Another tactic is to increase the speed of your speech and, for the moment, eliminate the pauses that give opportunities to interjectors. In a lively meeting, dramatic pauses should be avoided. They are manna from heaven to interjectors. Even more so are rhetorical questions.

The art of interjection lacks study and exposition in books about public speaking. This is unfortunate because in some meetings interjections can be very important indeed.

Firstly, from the interjector's point of view, he or she waits for the pause at the end of a badly expressed sentence, which will give him or her a chance to jump in. He or she especially waits to answer a rhetorical question. In a lively meeting, it is dangerous to ask such questions.

The interjector has to think quickly and make his or her statement loudly and in as few words as possible. The object of the exercise may be simply to amuse everyone, but it is more likely to be the humiliation, even the destruction, of the speaker.

How should the speaker react in the very, very short time in which it is possible to react? When in doubt, press on; pause a little perhaps if the audience is laughing, but press on as quickly as possible. Do not lose your temper; join in the laughter if it is not too inconsistent with your theme. If it is so inconsistent, preserve a straight face and press on as soon as the laughter fades. Do not delay lest there be another interjection.

A useful resource for the speaker subjected to interjections is to target the interjector. One simple way is to ask who it was that interjected, but if you do ask and the interjector replies you are rather expected by the audience to have a good reply. You have gained a little time to think by asking who the interjector was, but not much.

Another method of targeting the interjector that I have seen used successfully is to point in the interjector's direction but go on with your speech. This usually silences the interjector for a few moments, but it is best if the speaker diverts from the speech to crush the interjector. This is not always possible. I have seen speakers, having continued with the speech, lower the arm pointing at the interjector, leaving that person effectively ignored, but this tactic only comes off sometimes.

Dealing with interjectors is difficult. You will win some and lose some, but if you keep your temper and press on, all will be well.

Provocation of a speaker by opposing speakers is unfortunately a part of tough meetings. An effective tactic by opponents is to accuse a speaker of being anti-feminist, anti-gay, anti-Muslim, pro-rapists, anti-Australian, pro-American, and so forth. There are numerous areas of especially political disputation where, if the speaker is careless, someone will raise one or more of the current slogans. If one is discussing a sensitive subject (such as false allegations of rape), great care needs to be taken so that a precise point of view is accurately stated, leaving no room for claims that the speaker has offended current politically correct speech. One has to be careful to minimise the opportunity for opponents to misrepresent what you have said.

It might be usefully added that when a speaker has made the point of the speech, the speech should end. Waffling on because you like the sound of your voice, or because you feel the speech should be longer or because you don't know how to conclude, is likely to lead to statements you regret.

From what I have said it is obvious that lively meetings are not for sensitive speakers. In fact politicians in particular should be thick-skinned but are often very sensitive, at least about their own feelings. If you are going to do a lot of public speaking it is best to get used to personal attacks and not get too upset about them.

Especially one should not bear resentment against people who attack you. It is much better to shrug your shoulders and press on, remembering that today's attacker may well be tomorrow's ally.

12.

Learning to make a persuasive speech

MANY PEOPLE HAVE THE ability to say 'a few well-chosen words' on appropriate occasions. This common expression is usually a gross misdescription of the speech which is anything but that. These days, one often hears speeches at weddings and funerals in particular from people who may normally have little to do with public speaking. They vary in quality. Facility with words while on your feet is, however, only a first step in persuasive speaking.

In this book, there are many warnings as to the possible mistakes and blunders that might be made by a would-be persuader. There are also a number of suggestions that I hope will assist in the preparation and delivery of a persuasive speech. Ultimately, though, persuasive speaking is learned the fool's way, by experience, often bitter experience. A book such as this, I hope, assists a learner, so that fewer mistakes will be made. But no preparation will prevent humiliation and disappointment arising out of attempts to persuade.

A barrister usually learns little from a success. If counsel is wise, thought will be devoted after the case to why success was achieved, and whether any new tactic or method was a success. But life is full and there are other cases.

On the other hand, when counsel loses a case, particularly one that was expected to be a winner, a great deal of thought will be devoted to the causes of defeat if he or she is wise. To oneself, one can be brutally frank and emphasise errors so that they will not be repeated. Of course, there may not have been any substantial errors; unexpected evidence may have changed the course of the proceedings, or perhaps one's expectations were in error.

Outside the courts, efforts at persuasive speaking do not succeed or fail in the same spectacular fashion as court cases. Nevertheless, the key to progress as a persuasive speaker is having a mental post-mortem after each speech. In the case of a Rostrum meeting, the speaker has the benefit of the critic's comments. However, the sternest critic should be yourself.

Polite or even sustained applause is not always a reliable guide to the success of a persuasive speech. An audience may be impressed and entertained, but still not convinced. The object of persuasion is to convince the audience. Reluctant or even grudging acceptance of your argument is better than applause.

To advance as a persuader, you should be your own sternest critic. This does not merely apply to a learner. It applies to any persuader, no matter how experienced. There is always something more to be learned.

Often enough, others will point out the faults in your arguments and sometimes the faults in your presentation. It is much nicer to accept praise than criticism, but you only learn from the latter. Learning the fool's way by experience, though, is not pleasant and it is desirable to avoid errors, rather than learn by making them.

Reading great speeches is useful. Even better is listening to tapes and videos of good speeches. It should be remembered that transcripts of great speeches are usually edited and even doctored, so that they are not quite the same as the actual speeches.

I stress that if one is going to quote from a speech made by someone else, one does so as a quote. Using the words as one's own is undesirable, even dishonest. In a bad case, it is plagiarism.

Learning from the speeches of others is an art in itself. Some things may be safely copied or adapted but you must remain yourself. If you try to be a John F. Kennedy you will look a fool, but you can learn a lot from his vivid phrases and sentences.

Of course, the important aspect of persuasive speaking is knowledge of the subject. Study of the subjects on which you intend to speak will lead to knowledge and knowledge will lead to confidence. Probably the basic characteristics of a good persuader are wide reading and eager acquisition of knowledge. Added to those are a knowledge of human nature and a genuine sympathy, even affection, for one's fellow mortals. You will do better as a persuader when you feel affection for your audience.

The weakness of Rostrum criticism was the reluctance of critics to examine the subject matter of speeches. Yet the subject matter of a speech is obviously the most important part. Unless you have something worthwhile to say, your speech will be useless and, no matter how well disguised by clever language and voice, it will appear to be useless. There is no substitute for substance, and the substance of a speech is its subject matter. That is why it is so essential to have a well-informed mind if you are to be a good speaker.

It is an unfortunate fact that the extent of modern knowledge is such that too much of one's learning time is occupied in simply learning how to make a living. Within the professions specialisation is now the rule, not the exception as it used to be. One is lucky to be able to self-educate oneself while studying for one's career. Yet self-education is essential and by this I mean acquiring knowledge outside one's profession or occupation.

There is a wonderful, almost limitless world of information to be found in books; perhaps even more is to be found on the internet, in the media, and in daily conversations. I have known doctors and dentists who were very well informed, largely through conversations with their patients. There are many ways of acquiring information. Conversation is one of the most important ways.

Of course verbal, internet and media information may be unreliable, as may be the information contained in books. These days, however, secondary and tertiary education is aimed at developing critical minds, much more so than when I was a boy.

If you are to be a good speaker, you must be well informed and this generally means that your education must continue throughout your life. Self-education may well be more important than school and university education. The point is that somehow a good speaker must acquire the information, reliable information, for his or her speeches.

Of course, there can be special reading and research for a prepared speech, but this does best when supported by a wealth of background knowledge. There are also many speeches that have to be made when there is little or no time for preparation, but it still pays to be well informed and interested in as many topics as possible. Although 'a little knowledge is a dangerous thing', no knowledge is worse. A good speaker goes through an endless process of learning.

It is only from a wide choice of facts that one can select those facts suitable for the particular speech. The subject of the speech may have already been chosen, but the selection of the detailed subject matter is the first and most important part of learning to make a speech. This may well take a great deal of time, often involving discarding one approach and taking another. Learning to select the subject matter involves practice. Although what convinces you in particular may not do so for your particular audience, perhaps with modification and adaptation it will.

In competitive speaking, whether debating or otherwise, you may have the benefit of an adjudicator's comments. These may be right or wrong as you see it, but you must always accept and examine the fact that your speech had that effect on that particular listener. It is unusual for an adjudicator's comments not to contain some useful assistance. Often the comments are very useful, as are the criticisms of Rostrum critics. A good speaker will usually learn from the criticisms of others, even bad criticism.

One can learn from audience reactions, and the comments of one's friends. Unfortunately, one's friends tend to give praise whether deserved or not, lest they offend you. However, if they realise that you will not be offended and want genuine criticism, you may well receive it.

As you progress, and learn more about public speaking, it may well be that you will become your own best critic. To improve, you should always conduct your own post-mortems – the more detailed the better.

Be careful about judging a speech by the applause. Some audiences are only too polite, and sometimes the applause will really be for your reputation, rather than the speech itself. Australian audiences are usually generous with applause. I have often noticed this at plays and operas when it is not uncommon for poor performances to be loudly applauded. Furthermore, applause can often be fairly easily obtained by quite simple tricks. A platitude that precisely coincides with the prejudices of a particular audience will get rounds of applause. I fear that political speechwriters have stores of these ready for the appropriate occasion. A careful sentence may be composed just to suit that audience and gain applause. That is really good persuasion but one should not be unduly carried away when it comes off. It is only part of the speech.

The cases over which I conducted lengthy mental post-mortems were my losses. Four years after I retired from fifty-two years as a barrister, the cases that return to my memory tend to be losses. There were quite a few of these.

Sometimes the case against the client was overwhelming and I struggled through to ultimate defeat.

The post-mortem was not so unpleasant but I wondered always if I could have done better, and, if so, how.

The bitter, mind-wrenching post-mortems were when one should have won but lost. I still remember vividly a case for a young Italian fisherman who was injured by a motor car when he was a pedestrian. Juries often decided such cases in those days, and this was a jury trial. The presiding judge summed up all my way but the verdict was for the defendant motorist.

My client was a very nice young gentleman. It was his case but he said to me afterwards, 'Don't worry, Mr Porter, you did your best.' This was an unusual reaction to say the least. Later he brought me a present of a splendid fish. (He still had his injured leg after the case. I do hope he managed to get by, and had a happy life.)

I was a very severe critic of myself in this case. I considered my opening address was too flowery. I was copying another counsel, and this is always dangerous. I wondered whether I had fully appreciated the strength of the defendant's case. I realised that I had failed to consider the situation from the defendant driver's viewpoint. If I was to successfully rebut this, I should have more closely examined it.

Was my cross-examination thorough enough? Had I taken a strong plaintiff's case too much for granted? Did I realise that a jury of people who drove their own cars would sympathise with the driver rather than the pedestrian? Had I put the jury offside in something I said?

Years later, with the benefit of many years' experience, I realised that my performance was hardly earth-shattering. I made many mistakes, but they were not very significant. The fact was, as I knew then, that the verdict was misguided. This was not that long after the war and one member of the jury hated Italians. I could see that that one juror certainly did not like the plaintiff and he was the strong man of the jury. The other three jurors (there are only four in civil cases) seemed unhappy but they went along. There seemed no logical reason why the plaintiff – a pleasant enough young man – should have put a juror offside, but there had been a war against Italy. Of course, even now I may be wrong about the reasons for this loss. One never really knows in these cases. But it is impossible to sleep peacefully after apparent injustice. A defeat can be bitter indeed.

When I won, the tendency was to feel good for a very short time, even boast to someone if a good friend was handy, and then devote myself to the next case. I realise now that this was a mistake, just as it is a mistake not to post-mortem a successful speech.

Sometimes a case is won despite the incompetence of counsel. It may have been a strong case or there may have been a large element of good luck. The same applies to speeches. A speech may have succeeded because the cause was popular and the audience was in a good mood. Success in a court case or a speech by no means guarantees that the presentation was perfect or even competent.

Obviously there is a tendency not to subject success to a post-mortem and it probably is not done as often as it should be. That was certainly so in my case. Yet there is obviously much to learn from a success. One should ask oneself the questions: what could I have done further, what mistakes did I make, and, especially, why did I succeed? If one finds that one has done something well, to re-examine it will make it that much more likely that you will do it again.

Some successes should be examined as failures simply because you should have failed and the success was due to good luck rather than the persuader's skill. Few successes are the result of perfect performance. Often, re-examination of a case will show how close you went to failure. The same may apply to any successful speech.

The fundamental point in learning to make a speech is, in most spheres of learning, that you must aim for perfection. You will never attain it, but the more you try, the more you will improve.

13.

Clear words

APART FROM BREVITY, TO call a spade a spade has an advantage of clarity over calling it 'a hand-held digging implement'.

In the 1930s, it was common to use euphemisms rather than direct words in the interests of delicacy. Thus there was a story told to young advocates of the pregnant lady who was caught red-handed shoplifting in a Sydney department store. In those days, shoplifting was regarded as a very serious offence, so that a first offender might very well be sent to gaol.

Still, it was widely believed that a pregnant lady might lose her inhibitions during the term and perhaps even steal. In any event, few magistrates would have relished the idea of sending a pregnant young lady to gaol. So her young counsel informed the bench that there were extenuating circumstances. His client, he said, was 'in a certain condition'.

This submission failed dismally. His Worship stated firmly that in his opinion drunkenness was not an excuse; in fact, it made the offence even more serious. The young lady made the descent to the cells below and later in the day was driven off to serve a sentence of six months' imprisonment.

Fortunately, the story ends happily. She appealed and her new counsel told the judge that his client was pregnant, a word which, far from shocking His Honour, secured his client's immediate release.

I remember that in a translation of Guy de Maupassant's *Short Stories* of that period, namely the decade between the wars, the word 'pregnant' never appeared, but there was a plentiful use of the French word '*enceinte*'. Apparently this was to protect the tender sensibilities of readers in the early twentieth century.

So it was in that time and up to the 1940s and 1950s, when I started to practise as a barrister, that little girls who were the subject of alleged sexual assault gave evidence of the touching of their 'private parts'. I sometimes wondered how many wretches did time for touching a little girl's neck or her arm or some other non-sexual portion of her body. By the 1960s, children referred to their sexual organs by their ordinary names without much embarrassment.

During this same time, every day one or more malefactors appeared in the dock of Central Police Court's charge court facing the charge of 'indecent language'. The language was written on a piece of paper so that no one was embarrassed by the words being read aloud and the paper was known as the 'language sheet'. As often as not, it was a simple admonition to the constable to go away using the word legitimised by D.H. Lawrence in *Lady Chatterley's Lover*. At the same time, it was stated that the constable was born out of wedlock.

When speaking to one or more persons, or an audience of many persons, the questions one must ask oneself are, 'Why should they listen?' and 'Is anything I'm saying stopping them listening?' Long polysyllables may well make the speaker appear learned and wise, but the audience may not understand the fine language. In fact, polysyllables may well put an audience to sleep.

I can remember in my student days studying a book on jurisprudence with a dictionary beside me so that I could look up words that I could not understand. An audience has neither a dictionary nor the time to consult one. So, if the speaker displays his or her long vocabulary, there will be a lost audience, which first fails to understand, and then ceases to listen.

If a lawyer or a doctor addresses a lay audience,

professional jargon is best forgotten, so that the words used can be understood.

It is surprising how effective the use of simple words can be. This was well appreciated by both Winston Churchill and Franklin D. Roosevelt, the great leaders in the Second World War. Churchill achieved great effect by calling Adolf Hitler 'that bad man', and I remember Roosevelt's 'Lend-Lease' speech before America entered the war in aid of a desperate Britain: 'Britain needs planes; from America she will get [pause] planes. Britain needs ships; from America she will get [pause] ships . . .' and so on. I remember a speech by Bob Hillman, a very good Rostrum speaker, in which he said, 'There has been blood on the mat at Rushcutter's Bay Stadium, and the crowd loved it.' In a few simple words he conjured up a vivid scene, illustrative of an important aspect of human nature. Boxing can be horrible, as can be football, but even sophisticated modern man has his primitive side.

The skilful use of simple words is an essential attribute of advocates who practise before juries in criminal cases. When I was defending Judge John Foord, I referred to him (with great accuracy) as 'the man who was shot down in someone else's war'. This summed up the whole story of a misguided prosecution of a good man charged with attempting to pervert the course of justice.

It is a pity that in many sections of the media today there is a deliberate avoidance of a simple direct message.

This is not done by complicated or polysyllabic language but rather by 'beating around the bush' with the use of obscure messages. The idea is that the audience of cinema or television advertisements will strain to understand what on earth is being advertised and how to obtain it. In many cases, the audience does not bother to try; in others it tries but fails to understand.

I suppose that if one pays money to see a film or a play, one will strain to understand what it is all about. One may even think that one is being very clever understanding or thinking one understands the message. This is particularly so with regard to American crime films or novels (for example, novels by Raymond Chandler). The plots are, to say the least, contrived, complicated, unlikely and not true to life. It is a form of entertainment to watch what seems to happen and hope to understand what actually did happen.

However, I believe that if one is trying to persuade one or more persons or an audience the obscure 'guess what I am driving at?' approach is to be avoided. It is true that some people will strive to understand and be triumphant when they do or think they do. This is rather like an addiction to crossword puzzles. It may even be that those who do understand are likely to be convinced. But, as I said before, the vast majority of listeners switches off to such an approach and ceases to listen. Others will try to understand and fail. They will blame the speaker, not themselves, for this failure.

I do not think it is fair to say that the average audience is intellectually lazy. Nevertheless, people have other things to do than listen to you. They have busy lives, and often have a lot on their minds. If you are obscure, why should they bother to try to understand, or even listen?

Even an audience such as a jury or a committee or a company board does not want to be played with by obscure sentences that eventually may lead somewhere. Committees and company boards may well lack the patience to follow and understand obscure and very subtle submissions.

A jury would much prefer to acquit and looks to the counsel for the accused to give them an excuse to acquit. (I am indebted to the late Judge Alfred Goran and the late Judge Trevor Martin for the wisdom contained in this last sentence.) When an acquitting jury returns to court, one can often see quite clearly happy, relieved faces. The jurors look at the accused, sometimes in a very friendly 'you'll be right, mate' fashion. On the other hand, convicting juries often avoid looking at the accused. They appear unhappy and, not infrequently, female jurors are crying. Of course, when the evidence is very clear and the offence nasty, one can sometimes come across a self-righteous convicting jury, which returns smug-faced and superior. This is a 'we've fixed you' jury.

In some cases, the Crown evidence fails and the accused is obviously innocent, so the jury is happy to acquit. In other cases, the Crown evidence is overwhelming and the accused should have pleaded guilty. (A plea of guilty usually results in a lesser sentence.) In most cases, there is room for argument and the object of a good defence counsel is to give the jury an excuse to acquit. This excuse is best and most effectively contained in a simple submission in simple words.

Sometimes the excuse to acquit is complicated and may require detailed explanation. The art then is to make the explanation as simple as possible and therefore as convincing as possible. This does not mean that the address should not be accompanied by illustrations, even anecdotes, to make it more interesting. It is, of course, much easier to understand an argument if it is illustrated by example or stories. But the message, the central message, should be effectively expressed in simple words. The idea of such an address is that everyone should understand it with as little mental effort as possible. You do not make such an address in terms that only the cute and clever people can understand. You do not try to display your own enormous vocabulary and learning. You do not use words that may require the listener to reach for a dictionary.

And of course, as I've previously mentioned, beware of euphemisms. They are useful for witty or sarcastic speeches and writings. They are dangerous to use in serious efforts to persuade.

There is one qualification to all I have said. One trick of persuasion is to make the audience think of the argument for itself, or at least think that it has done so. Sometimes in an address to a jury, the facts and arguments are marshalled in a way where one or more of the jury will reach a conclusion and think they got there by themselves. It is human nature to be persuaded by one's own arguments.

It is difficult, but by no means impossible, to feed an argument to an audience without stating it. If that audience then thinks that it very cleverly thought up that argument, it is likely to find its own argument very convincing.

This is a great tactic if it comes off. If it does not come off, in most cases the argument should reach the audience, even if not as its own argument. The obvious danger is that because of this tactic the speaker will be too clever by half and the argument will be missed altogether. This is a real danger, and only a very experienced persuader with a real appreciation of the audience should attempt this tactic.

With this dangerous exception, the message should always be at least summed up and repeated in simple terms and simple words.

There is a great power in simplicity and a very great power in simple words.

14.

Playing the trump card

EFFECTIVE PERSUASION IS DEPENDENT upon careful and often prolonged consideration of the subject matter. A good advocate may spend many hours in preparation, not so much reading and re-reading the relevant material but in thinking about it.

J.T. Hiatt QC, when leading me in the second Voyager Royal Commission in 1967, told me several times to come to his chambers and confer about the case without any brief or papers, to just think about the case, and discuss where we were going and what we should do. He was right. Although careful consideration of the material is essential by reading and digesting it, once it has been digested, poring over it yet again serves little purpose. One must think about it.

Almost inevitably, this cogitation should produce one's trump card, one's best point or argument, and, in the case of cross-examination, the likely cracking point of the opposition's key witness.

Thus arises one of the controversial questions of advocacy. When does one put forward the best argument; when does one ask the key question? Advocates disagree about this, and I should be the first to concede that a lot may depend upon the circumstances.

Nevertheless, as a general rule I am of the opinion that one should play the trump card early. It may be that there needs to be some introduction, some softening up perhaps, but in my experience the longer the playing of the trump card is delayed, the less effective it becomes.

I remember a case in which I appeared many years ago before the late Justice Dennis Needham, one of our best equity judges, who had a great reputation as a barrister and as a judge. The other party claimed to be a doctor of philosophy and used the title 'doctor' often, verbally and in writing. He was a good witness and likely to be very hard to crack on the essentials of a difficult equity suit. My solicitors had made inquiries of the university where he was supposed to have acquired his title and it had no record of him acquiring a doctorate, or even having attended the university. This university was overseas and its letter, without much more, was not admissible in evidence.

This witness finished his evidence in chief fairly early in the afternoon. There was a great deal of matters that my clients denied but this would simply be word against word. My clients claimed to have been double-crossed, but the witness had an excellent front.

To everyone's surprise, I opened my cross-examination on the subject of his doctorate, asking how he had acquired it, and when. He confidently answered the questions firmly, and with some pride in his academic achievement. Without reading the university's letter aloud (which I could not do under the rules of evidence), I showed him the letter. I then asked him whether he still maintained he was a doctor. He said he did.

I then went into a lengthy cross-examination as to how there had to be a certificate for his doctorate, would he produce it, where was it and so on. Would a person coming to Australia to live and practise his profession leave such an important certificate in Europe? If not, where was it? We adjourned the hearing at 4 pm.

Next morning at 10 am, the cross-examination continued, but he had obviously considered overnight the consequences of perjury. He decided his best course was to confess and hope for the best. He admitted that he was not a doctor and that yesterday's evidence was false. There was an adjournment and we settled the case on very favourable terms. The witness's credit had been destroyed before my witnesses had been heard and before there was any cross-examination about the issues in the case.

Both counsel later had morning tea with Dennis Needham, a most friendly and hospitable judge. Of course the atmosphere of an equity suit would very rarely even approach the tension of a criminal trial.

Dennis Needham remarked to me how he often wondered why counsel delayed their best shot. He completely agreed with my having fired it first of all and incidentally saving a lot of valuable court time.

Had I delayed my trump card and cross-examined the other issues, it would not have had anything like the same effect. It would simply have been a successful part of a cross-examination that was only good in part.

It is the same for a trump card argument as it is for cross-examination. I am firmly of the opinion that the trump card should be played first, that is, the best argument should come first. In ordinary one-on-one conversation, why not start with the best argument? Why risk initial rebuttal when you commence with your next best arguments (which are often not good enough)?

When arguing before a company board, a committee or a bench of judges such as the High Court of Australia or the Court of Appeal, the great temptation is to do everything so systematically and carefully that the main argument is obscured. I suppose most advocates are anxious to ensure that they put forward every possible argument for the client. Often a judgment commences, 'Mr Bloggs has put forward (very capably) every possible argument on behalf of his client.' This is known as the kiss of death, because it says, in effect, that Mr Bloggs has lost his case. It would be a far greater tribute to Mr Bloggs to say that he put his best argument as forcefully and skilfully as possible. You may, of course, have two, even three, best arguments, but, if they all fail, what hope is there in dredging up numerous futile arguments doomed to failure? Remember, however, that careful thought should have sifted out the best arguments. Unfortunately many persuaders, even barristers, have no idea what or which is or are their best argument or arguments.

I concede the possibility of there being three apparently best arguments. The likelihood is that there will be one only, rarely two. If one good argument succeeds, it hardly matters if there are other arguments that might have succeeded. To dredge up every possible argument may be necessary in a situation where the good arguments have failed. Sometimes a seemingly hopeless argument succeeds. Sometimes you may have made a bad classification of your possible arguments. However, dredging up every possible argument is a counsel of desperation in an apparently hopeless situation.

Let me stress again that the preliminary exercise is to sort out the possible arguments and select the best one. Possibly there will be one or two runners-up. Then advance that argument as early and as efficiently as possible. It may be necessary to open up the subject, but all the time the build-up should be to the main argument that will win the day.

Some years ago, I appeared in an appeal from a decision of the Land and Environment Court to the New South Wales Court of Appeal. At first instance, the case had gone for weeks and my client had lost. The case was then reopened for a further lengthy hearing based on new evidence, but again my client failed. So far I had not appeared in the matter, but my junior on the appeal had appeared throughout. We had to prepare pages of written submissions on the appeal, which was set down for a hearing of either two or three days, a long hearing time for an appeal.

Nevertheless, after a lot of consideration of the case, to me there seemed to be a simple trump-card argument. At first instance, a test, wrong in law, had been applied to the evidence. On that I came to a firm conclusion. Then I applied what I considered to be the correct test to all the evidence and, as I saw it, there was no evidence to support the finding against my client. I very carefully prepared this one point and left the reserve points on the side to be argued only if the main point failed. The appeal took only half a day and succeeded on the one point.

This approach does not only apply to appeals and

arguments on questions of law. It applies to questions of fact, testing the crucial facts.

When I was counsel assisting the Morling Royal Commission concerning Lindy Chamberlain, from the vast body of forensic evidence it seemed to me that the crucial evidence was an alleged arterial blood spray in the Chamberlains' car. Whether it could be proved to be foetal blood (baby's blood) or not, there was no suggested innocent explanation for such a blood spray.

Les Smith, a scientist working on behalf of the Chamberlains, had already cast considerable doubt on this blood spray since the trial. Tony Raymond of the Victorian Forensic Science Laboratory rang me after examining the spray at my request. At the laboratory, I looked through a microscope at his direction. The alleged blood spray had flecks of duco sprayed on top of it. It turned out to be sound deadener sprayed in error during manufacture of the car.

Once that enormous forensic blunder was revealed, there was a very considerable weakening of the whole body of forensic evidence. Further errors were revealed and eventually the case against Mrs Chamberlain collapsed because the only evidence against her was forensic evidence. There were arguments about inconsistencies and contradictions in Lindy Chamberlain's own evidence, but otherwise all the non-forensic evidence was strongly in her favour.

The under-dash alleged blood spray was a key starting point.

It is, of course, systematic to present one's arguments in chronological order. This may well ensure that no possible argument is missed, but, as I have stressed already, the object should be to present the successful argument, not every possible argument.

However, this concept should not be carried too far. The best argument, or the crucial evidence, can only be ascertained after a thorough examination of all relevant materials, whether evidential or, in a legal case, legal.

One can only find the trump card in the context I have been discussing by careful examination of, and cogitation over, everything relevant. If you think you have found the trump card, you must carefully examine it and consider it in the context of everything relevant to the questions under consideration. One must resist the temptation to jump to a conclusion on inadequate materials, or to omit considering everything relevant.

Finding the trump card may, in some contexts, be easy. In others, it may take a long while. The success of the trump card very much depends upon finding the correct card. However, once it has been ascertained with certainty, it should be played as early as possible.

First impressions are very important. To my mind, it is a grave mistake to create a poor impression by opening with a weak argument. The listener, having dismissed that argument, may well get into a dismissal habit and dismiss the trump card when it is played at last.

In summary, the idea should be to find the trump card (possibly with a runner-up or even two); ensure that it is, in fact, the trump card; and then concentrate on presenting it early, forcefully and efficiently.

If it fails, there may be one or two runner-up arguments and they should be presented next. If they fail, you can always fall back on the lesser arguments. You can ingeniously dredge up all possible arguments, receive the kiss of death from the judge, and then accept defeat gracefully.

As Sam Leibowitz, the famous New York attorney of the Scottsboro Boys fame, said to the only man he ever lost to the electric chair: 'You can't win them all.'

15.

Working with an ally

It often occurs in criminal cases that two persons are tried together as being both involved in the same offence. This can be an enormous advantage to the Crown. If they accuse each other, if they run the cut-throat defence of 'I did not, but he did', both will inevitably be convicted. I know of no exceptions to this simple proposition.

I had not been a barrister that long in the early 1950s when I was briefed to defend an alleged homosexual charged with indecent assault on his co-accused. Indecent touching between consenting males was an offence in those days.

My opponent was represented by a Mr X. (He died years ago but there is no point in naming him.) We agreed, as it was common sense to agree, that we should run in co-operation and neither should attack the other. After all, each denied guilt and therefore denied the police evidence. It might be observed that if one was guilty, the other could hardly be innocent.

I addressed the court first and then Mr X addressed. To my amazement, he invited the jury to convict my client and acquit his client. The jury could easily detect the double-cross, from my address and from my expression. Perhaps they heard me say 'You rat'. Of course both men were convicted, but, as I remember it, both got bonds and did not go to gaol. At least for first offenders, homosexuals were rarely sent to gaol, even in those days.

It was a nasty experience. Dirty double-crosses of this nature were fortunately rare at the bar, but they were not completely unknown. A defence counsel is by and large very rarely entitled to ask a jury to convict a co-accused. That is not his or her function. It is the wise convention among barristers practising criminal law not to interfere with or damage the case of a co-accused unless it is absolutely unavoidable. As I have said, cut-throat defences are a highway to conviction. There are no exceptions.

On the other hand, cooperation between allies can lead to success. Many years ago, a large public company failed and many people lost a lot of money. There were two auditors who were partners at the time and they were the obvious scapegoats in the disaster.

It was one of the many cases one finds in the law, and in ordinary life, where negligence is obvious enough with the wisdom of hindsight. Unfortunately, human nature being what it is, we are all negligent in all aspects of life, not excluding our professions if we hold ourselves out as professionals. The best of us make mistakes; the most careful often fail to see the obvious. Judges are frequently found to be wrong by the Court of Appeal, and Judges of Appeal are frequently found to be wrong by the High Court of Australia. We are all human.

Nevertheless, if a professional person makes a mistake, he or she may well be liable for heavy damages. Most mistakes have no dreadful consequences; a few do. That is why most professional persons have professional liability insurance policies; and in many professions such policies are compulsory.

A slight mistake by an obstetrician may result in a baby crippled for life, and an award of damages of ten million dollars or more. However that mistake is not classed as professional misconduct, which might cause the doctor to be struck off the medical registry. On the other hand, gross or reckless negligence would be serious professional misconduct for a doctor or any other professional person.

After the failure of the company, the two auditors quarrelled and their partnership was dissolved. Each now blamed the other for the debacle in the auditing of the company.

The Institute of Chartered Accountants, which is a private body regulating chartered accountants, charged both the accountants with professional misconduct. Des Ward, a barrister at the time, later a judge, was briefed to defend one; I was briefed to defend the other. I had had, even then, quite a lot of experience in appearing before professional disciplinary tribunals, but Des Ward was an older, senior, and more experienced barrister than I. We worked well together; he was clever and cooperative.

Both our clients were told very firmly that they would sink or swim together, that the slightest attack on the other was the first step on the road to disaster for both. With some difficulty, we persuaded our clients to comply with our advice. Then we agreed that in order to make the best presentation and avoid any possible conflict, or even contradiction between our clients, Des Ward would present the arguments on the facts and I would address on the law. Obviously, we discussed both aspects together.

The Institute of Chartered Accountants is a large body of persons and the evidence before them had largely been collected and collated in written form before the hearing. This hearing was mainly addresses on evidence. It was efficient and fair.

Des Ward addressed very well and analysed the evidence skilfully and effectively. I addressed to explain the difference between mere negligence and professional misconduct. The result was that the professional charges against both men were dismissed.

I have discussed this case in detail because it demonstrates the main rules applicable to co-defences. These are:

1. Do not attack each other.
2. Do not contradict each other.
3. Use the combined wisdom of both counsel in the interests of both the accused persons.
4. Cooperate and discuss to ensure compliance with rules 1, 2, and 3.

The same rules apply to longer cases, too, and is illustrated by a double murder case involving two accused in which I appeared not so long ago. The co-accused was represented by Robert Somosi, a very capable junior counsel, much younger than me. Robert's emotional temperament was rather different from mine, but we got on well. As the case progressed, I developed an enormous respect for his ability. He was quite a genius in some respects, although at times he tended to be hasty and impetuous. I suppose I was cautious. We had our disputes but we resolved them. We always presented a united consistent front. On one occasion, Robert's client said to him loud enough for me to hear, 'Don't offend the old man'. This was some years ago and was hardly complimentary to me but it achieved its purpose. Our united front succeeded.

Alliances between experienced counsel are one thing. Alliances in politics and meetings are quite different. No one likes to be told what to do; no one likes to be restrained. We all want to do our own thing in our own way. Perhaps some of us want to get the lion's share of the credit, we may want to show off, we may want media publicity. All of these things mitigate from a successful working alliance.

Furthermore, alliances come and go. One moment someone is on your side, the next he or she is off on a lone mission or on a different cause.

On a committee or a company board or in a public meeting, alliances tend to be temporary, undisciplined and uncontrolled. Thus allied supporters of a cause contradict each other and often undermine each other. Yet unity is strength and a united approach is much more likely to succeed than a divided one. Division is weakness, and the high road to defeat in most aspects of life, but most certainly in politics.

To avoid division, the Labor Party from its earliest days bound members to caucus decisions. Some say the party went too far, but splits and divisions have always been the bane of the left side of politics. Hence the stern discipline to achieve unity.

A politician averse to compromise is almost certain to fail. There are too many differences and shades of opinion even among members of the same political party.

Alliances are essential to achieve success for a cause. Compromise is essential in order to achieve a successful alliance. So if someone wants to support you but has one or two reservations, there is an obvious need to discuss those reservations. The problems can often be solved by a compromise that makes no sacrifice of principle. That is what should be done if there is time available.

Unfortunately, often there is not time available and allies or potential allies only reveal themselves at the meeting. Often enough they support you publicly, but with public reservations.

When this occurs, you should seize gratefully the support offered and deal politely and tactfully with the reservations. It is surprising how often I have heard speakers do just the opposite. Yet who can afford to say to the world 'Support me one hundred percent or oppose me'? The answer to that is obvious.This is particularly important in small meetings involving committees, company boards or local councils. One vote may make all the difference. Every effort should be made to secure it.

In courtroom alliances, it is usually found that differences of tactics and approach can be easily solved after friendly discussion. It is the same with meeting alliances. Reservations and/or minor differences can usually be resolved, if not immediately then later.

Where your supporter disagrees with you on some aspect, the best approach to the problem is to hear him or her out, at length if necessary. In the end, you may find that you agree with the reservations stated, once you fully understand them.

In conclusion, the fundamental rules for working successfully with an ally are:

1. Achieve unity if you possibly can.
2. Do not be hasty to reject a potential ally simply because the support offered is not one hundred per cent.
3. Resolve differences by compromise if you possibly can.
4. If there are differences between you and your ally, be tactful, and minimise the area of dispute.

In this world, there is not that much we can achieve on our own, unassisted. Accordingly, an important part of the art of persuasion is the careful handling of allies and potential allies. It is especially important to hear your potential ally out, before you part as opponents. Perhaps the attributes that will help you most are tact and understanding.

16.

The tricks of a public meeting

THIS CHAPTER IS INTENDED to assist in your understanding of what is meant to go on at a public meeting, and the role of persuasion.

The public meeting achieves its purpose by expressing its will in motions that, when passed as resolutions, reflect the wills of the majority present at the meeting. A persuader achieves the desired purpose of the persuasion by having passed a suitable resolution.

The chairperson presides, his or her objective being not simply to keep order but to ensure that the debates and discussions result in resolutions. Otherwise the purpose of the meeting is not achieved or, simply put, it wastes its time in useless chatter. This can occur with a weak chairperson.

The chairperson is supposed to be impartial in a true sense, not like the speaker of a parliament who is only truly impartial when the person holding the office is a person of exceptional integrity. In political parties, the chairperson is the president of the convention, conference or branch, and is usually very interested in the results achieved by the meeting. The same would apply to a chairperson of directors or the president of a club. They are supposed to be impartial at meetings but at the same time they have a duty to guide and lead the meeting.

One way of achieving a desired result is the selection of speakers. No one is entitled to speak until given the call by the chairperson. Assuming, for example, that the chairperson wishes a motion to be lost, he or she will give the call to the strongest speakers to be seen in the opposition, and the weakest to be seen in support. In fact, if he or she can find a hopeless ratbag to support the motion, then the defeat of the undesired motion is half achieved. Very frequently only a few of the persons wishing to speak can do so because of time restraints. Of course, by the rules, the mover and seconder of the motion must be called because they are respectively the propounder and first supporter of that motion.

Back in the late 1940s, when I, as a young member of the Liberal Party, opposed the plan to suppress the Communist Party and make being a communist a criminal offence, I seconded a motion to reject this plan (a plan which by then was Party policy) at the annual convention. Later I saw it as quite a compliment to myself that I was quite wrongly not called upon to speak by the president, the chairman of the meeting, even though I should have been because I was a seconder. Every strong speaker against the motion easily obtained the call, and every weak speaker for the motion was quickly given the call and there was only time for a comparatively few speakers. I took a point of order, and was then called to speak. I made quite a good speech, but on this occasion the lovers of liberty were in the minority and we lost. But, as R.L. Stevenson said, 'To struggle mightily is a better thing than to arrive.' Perhaps.

This trick of selection of speakers is widely employed, not least of all by the media. In a feature discussing a controversial question on TV, it is sometimes not hard to detect which side is favoured by the ABC. That side has a strong, able speaker whereas the opposition speaker would appear to be chosen for his or her incompetence and stupidity. But, of course, both sides have been heard, and afforded equal time.

It is a very old trick and no doubt Themistocles employed it to persuade the Athenian assembly that the people should leave Athens during the Persian War and go to Salamis. If I am right, this may be an example of the end justifying the means.

Another meeting manoeuvre to oppose a speaker is the frivolous point of order. I have already dealt in detail with interjections, but points of order are something else altogether. Technically, once a point of order is raised, the speaker should take a seat while the chairperson rules on the point. This completely interrupts the speech and may disrupt the speaker's chain of thought.

If the point is obviously frivolous, the speaker might well keep standing until the chairperson rejects it. In any event, where there is a meeting that tends to enforce rules, care should be taken not to infringe a rule. In particular, if a speaker wanders somewhat off the point, a point of order to the effect that the speaker is not speaking to the motion may perhaps succeed, and may well humiliate the speaker. Chairpersons usually permit some latitude about speaking to the motion, but if the point is taken, even if it fails, there may well be a comment from the chair inviting the speaker to keep to the point. This is humiliating and obviously does not improve the effective impact of the speech.

Another tactic to defeat a motion is to move multiple amendments. Experience shows that few chairpersons have the knowledge and experience to deal with multiple amendments. The books on chairmanship are not always unanimous about what the chairperson ought to do. With any luck, and perhaps some skill on the part of the opponents, a motion that should have been carried is either lost or amended into something useless in pursuing the objectives of the original mover.

Yet another tactic to defeat a motion is the frivolous amendment that is aimed at destroying the original motion. One quite common version of this is where there is a proposal to confer privileges on the wives of some persons. A good and true example is the proposal to confer conjugal rights upon prisoners, so as to preserve as far as possible the family ties that may be crucial in the prisoners' rehabilitation. How do you kill this not completely unreasonable motion?

You may want to say that prison is not meant to be a holiday, that it may be hard on wives, but prisoners must be punished. But that argument may not succeed, so you get 'A' to move that the privilege should also apply to de facto partners. While the meeting worries how far this may go, 'B' then moves that the privilege shall also apply to homosexual partners thereby introducing a completely new controversy which would produce strong opposition. When the chaos and confusion die down, those who were inclined to vote for the motion have changed their minds and that reform is never effected.

This is part of a wider tactic. If you oppose a privilege, say, to disabled pensioners, you then move an amendment to apply it to all pensioners and then another amendment is moved to apply to self-funded pensioners and, of course, ultimately the original motion is lost because the privilege would be much too expensive if applied to too many people.

Those persuaders who seek to reform a world that certainly needs to be reformed should know what they are up against. Knowledge is strength. I once succeeded in securing a privilege for members' widows in a society by explaining, when the usual de facto partners/homosexual partners tactic was tried, exactly what the purpose and result of such amendments were, namely to confuse the original issue and arouse opposition which would not apply to wives or widows.

I have already discussed working with allies. I once helped to achieve a very important amendment to the constitution of the Liberal Party by an alliance with Ray Watson QC. I put up reasons for the amendment and then there was an eruption of opposing speakers. Then, as planned, when the opponents had just about talked themselves out, Ray stood up to speak for the motion, but in particular to destroy the arguments against it. This he did most effectively and the motion was carried.

From this it may be observed that it may be important at a meeting to try to pick the time when you speak, whether before or after the opposition is apparent. Some speakers are excellent proposers of a motion; some are excellent destroyers of opposition. In important cases, support for or opposition against a motion is most effective when it is organised with your allies beforehand.

Usually the rules of a meeting provide for a right of reply. In fact, where there are no rules, the right of reply is zealously preserved by most participants at meetings. It seems to be regarded as a basic right, even after 'the gag' terminating the debate has been carried.

Only a few speakers use this very valuable right well. It is an extremely important speech; it is the last say before the vote. The right belongs to the mover of the motion but that mover can pass the right to another speaker if he or she so desires. At a Liberal Party conference a university motion attacking the recent actions of the Liberal state government appealed to me. It sought to ensure decisions on principle rather than expediency. I supported it, apparently so effectively that I was asked to make the speech in reply. We nearly, very nearly, succeeded in censuring the government at its own party conference. Perhaps this story explains why I was not a great success as a party member.

The speech in reply has two purposes: to sum up the case for the motion, and to rebut the arguments raised by the opponents of the motion. Technically the speech should not raise new arguments in favour of the motion, but a good speaker can make these flow from the arguments of the opposition so as not to be new matters at all.

If you are experienced in the affairs of meetings, and you have moved a motion that strikes opposition, you will be noting, either physically or mentally, the arguments against your proposal. You will be preparing your right of reply. If you can conclude on a powerful and effective note, what you say will be the last impression registering with the meeting.

Some speakers like to use the reply for a vigorous attack on the opposition. That is quite permissible and may be effective. It is important to observe a basic rule. *You may attack the argument but not the speaker.*

Personal attacks are usually counterproductive. They are rude, mean and usually unfair and unjust. Someone is quite entitled to think differently from you without having to put up with a personal attack. Sometimes, particularly in the political arena, personal attacks earn loud cheers and applause. They also create enmities that last for years.

It is possible to be very effective and also amusing and entertaining in crushing opposition arguments. You will be cheered and applauded. However, you should consider friendly refutation that appreciates the concerns of the opposition and then suggests why those concerns are not so serious or can be avoided. Such an approach will not achieve the same applause but is usually much more effective. Unfortunately so many people have trained as school-boy or -girl debaters or university debaters where smart rudeness earned cheers, that the art of gentle persuasion is rare. Once you master the art of gentle persuasion you will acquire respect and influence at meetings way beyond that of the clever show-offs.

Gentle persuasion is especially linked to the concept of giving your opponent an honourable way out, enjoying victory without humiliating the opposition. To acquire the art of gentle persuasion, you must cultivate the ability to understand the opposition and the patience to exercise that ability. This involves giving the opposition a careful and sympathetic hearing. Sometimes this will change your own mind. Often it will lead to a reasonable compromise. Otherwise you will be able to rebut effectively what you clearly understand, but the rebuttal will be sympathetic and friendly. On the next question, your opponent this time may well be your supporter.

If you take an active part in the proceedings of meetings, you will win some and lose some. You will often not get your own way. You should be careful to accept defeat gracefully. However, it is even more difficult to win gracefully, without giving offence.

In big gambling games winning gracefully is much more difficult than losing gracefully. This is worth pondering.

17.

Telling stories

MOST OF US HAVE some familiarity with the gospels of Jesus Christ, the teaching of which has had such a profound effect upon humankind. Many of these teachings were in the form of parables, only a few of which were actually explained by Jesus. The parable of the sower whose seed fell in various places was explained by Jesus and is thus a very clear example of a parable. The parable of the Good Samaritan was not explained but its meaning is clear enough. Other parables are not so clear and are open to interpretation.

These gospels are the greatest examples of persuasion by stories. The interest of the story retains the memory of the message.

Modern speakers rarely speak in parables, but stories are often used to illustrate and explain a point. There are numerous advantages in the use of stories.

Firstly, telling a story is the easiest way to make a speech. A speech in story form falls into place easily. And the words come without difficulty.

Secondly, a story is a very easy way to obtain audience attention. Everyone likes to hear a good story.

Thirdly, a story explains a proposition with a stirling simplicity difficult to achieve otherwise. Thus the duty to our neighbours is wonderfully explained in the parable of the Good Samaritan.

Fourthly, a story is long remembered. We can all vividly remember the fairy tales of our childhood.

In former years, an educated person was expected to know many, many stories. Billy Hughes, in one of his memoirs, maintained that no one was educated until he or she had read the Bible from cover to cover at least twice – or was it three times? I know of no one today who has performed this feat.

Stories in speeches are of two kinds, the well known and the new. After the Renaissance, the education of a cultured person included a detailed knowledge of the myths and legends of Ancient Rome and Greece. This knowledge is not so common today, so as a result mythical allusion can fall flat.

In speeches of yesterday, it was common to refer to

Bible stories or classical myths, confident that the listeners were familiar with them. These days, there cannot be the same confidence, even for the events of recent times such as D-day, the Berlin airlift, or the assassination of John F. Kennedy. Sometimes sports stories from tennis, cricket or football are familiar to most listeners. The trouble is that people are interested in different sports. Still, a reference to an Olympic star as well known as Ian Thorpe should connect easily with most audiences.

The reference to a familiar story in a speech should be brief, but enough to revive the complete story in the minds of the audience. Such a reference can be used very effectively to gain audience contact and to illustrate a proposition. Some biblical references such as the Good Samaritan and the sower are still effective with most audiences. Old Testament references to King Solomon or the parting of the Red Sea are likely to be familiar to a modern audience. (However, I was surprised to find during the Chamberlain Royal Commission how few people were familiar with the story from the Book of Daniel of the three men who endured the fiery furnace.)

These familiar tales are generally used as quick references to illustrate a point. Much more detail is given of a story which the audience does not know, or which it is believed that they do not know. When in doubt, it is possible to tell one of these familiar tales quickly for the benefit of the ignorant, but so as not to annoy those who know the story well. A speaker should remember that it is very annoying to listen to the re-telling of a story that most of the audience know, when the speaker believes that it is a new story. One thus needs to take care that a story told at length is, in fact, a new story.

The story should link up with the subject of a speech so as to form a useful part of that speech. It should illustrate and emphasise the point of the speech rather than submerge it. The danger in telling a lengthy story is that the speech will have no point or lose the point it had. Provided that this danger is borne in mind, it is possible to have a speech consisting almost entirely of the story that succeeds in making the point desired.

Should the speaker enter into the story straight away without any introduction or should the speaker make the point and then illustrate it with the story? In the former case, the point is made right at the end so that throughout the speech the audience wonders what the point may be right to the end when it is finally revealed. Some speakers love to keep the audience in suspense as to what the point will be, and often it comes off, but the climax must be worthwhile. The danger is that people will cease to care, or that the point that finally emerges will come as an anti-climax and the audience will feel cheated.

Storytelling is a great way to learn fluency and gesture. The speech flows with the story and gesture comes naturally. New speakers can often obtain greater confidence by telling stories from their own lives. If the story is about the speaker's humiliation, it is almost sure to get a good reception. People like to hear about the misfortunes (not too great) of others.

Otherwise, how does one find a good story? Sometimes it can be made up for the speech. One can then be confident that it has not been heard before. Sometimes it comes from history, sometimes directly from a book. In the latter case, the source should be acknowledged.

It is possible to tell a story that really impresses by learning off by heart a great piece of vivid writing and using the exact words as one's own. Of course, this is cheating and in a university would be serious academic misconduct. But I have seen it done, several times, and it was successful, at first, until the stolen passages were recognised and the speaker was humiliated. The temptation to do this should be resisted.

Many good stories come from wide reading, which is, of course, a very useful attribute for a speaker to have.

Some people are born raconteurs. With others, the art has to be developed. When you are beginning, it is probably best to tell the tale without too much elaboration, but as your skill develops, a plain tale can be decorated into a work of art.

You should seek to discover the interest in the story. This is a journalistic skill, to appreciate what is newsworthy to as many people as possible.

Many have criticised the novels of Charles Dickens by claiming that his characters are caricatures, not real people. I have always thought that this criticism completely misses the real point. Dickens had some experience as a journalist and powers of keen observation. When he met an unusual person whose very character was news, that person was remembered, given a not-altogether-usual name, and immortalised as a Ralph Nickleby (in *Nicholas Nickleby*), or a Sam Weller (in *The Pickwick Papers*) or even a Pumblechook (in *Great Expectations*). Perhaps the real genius of Dickens was his appreciation of what was news, or interesting to his audience, a very wide audience that ranged from workers to aristocrats.

The secret of successful storytelling is the ability to judge what will be interesting to the audience, and then to tell it in an interesting way. The story should contain a moral, or a lesson. The audience appreciates this. It makes the whole exercise worthwhile. Thus the story of the last native wolf or thylacine which died in Hobart Zoo in 1936, after bounties had been paid for killing thylacines in the wild, leads naturally to the lesson to protect our native fauna while there is time.

If you are wondering how much detail to put into a story, the answer is twofold. Will the detail add to the interest, and will it advance or detract from the point of the speech?

It is best to pick a story that appeals to you, because, if it does, your feeling for the story will emerge in the very tone of your voice. If you are going to tell a story that appeals to you, firstly reflect upon the question whether the story only appeals to you or should appeal to the audience. However, with experience you will learn to make what interests you interesting to almost everyone.

When Dickens gave his readings to enormous audiences, who paid well for the privilege of hearing him, he was reading from his favourite passages of his own novels. His feelings for the fate of his fictitious characters was such as to almost overwhelm both himself and the audience. Dickens was an astute judge of public interest and taste.

Few people understand Einstein's theory of relativity, and few care about it, but a good speaker on that apparently rather dull topic can make an audience enraptured with the subject matter. Many good topics, like good medicine, need a spoonful of sugar, but with that addition appeal to a wide audience.

I conclude this chapter with the warning that the story should not submerge the message of the speech. Do not be carried away as a mere raconteur, rather than a speaker with a message.

There is a great art in telling stories, but, although a lot can be learned from listening to good raconteurs, essentially each speaker must do his or her own thing.

R.G. Menzies was, I believe, one of the greatest of after-dinner speakers, especially as a raconteur. His voice and his features, particularly his bushy eyebrows, were remarkably expressive of what he was saying. It is probably a mistake to repeat one of his stories. Without his skill, it will fall flat.

In the end, you have to tell the story your way. With practice, that way will improve.

Often the temptation is to tell a funny story. That is a special skill in itself, as I shall discuss next.

18.

Humour

WITH MY APOLOGIES FOR misquoting Leon Gellert:

> Though some complain of life and scoff
> We all would like to laugh it off.

Most philosophers expand, perhaps too far, on the misery of human life. The media bring the misfortunes of the farthest and remotest parts of the earth into our lounge rooms per television and on to our breakfast tables per the newspapers. It is not as though our own lives are always happy. If we are not in trouble, our friends and relatives are. There is a lot of misery around.

Thus it is that the person who can make us laugh wins our affections. The speaker who has his or her audience laughing after the first few sentences can be sure of a sympathetic hearing thereafter. Humour is a powerful tool in the hands of a good speaker. Furthermore, if a speaker is really proficient in making an audience laugh, it is also probable that he or she can, within a few sentences, have that same audience sad and emotional.

However, modern audiences are not so volatile as those of yesterday. The late Clive Evatt KC has been described as having the presiding judge swaying like an entranced cobra, with the all male jury loudly weeping. This would be about an injured worker, or a bereaved worker's widow, seeking damages in a civil case. It is rare indeed today, though, to see an audience crying, although a good speaker can transfer the mood from laughter to subdued seriousness in a very short time.

Once the speaker has the audience laughing, they are friends ready to listen carefully to every word. It is hard to overstate the power of humour to a speaker.

Yet humour has its dangers. It can carry away the speaker as well as the audience, as once occurred to the famous George Reid, Premier of New South Wales and one of our earliest Prime Ministers. As a barrister, he was appearing for a plaintiff who had been a bride in a big social wedding that was ruined by the bungling of caterers. Apparently this bungling produced a chaos that George found amusing. As he was opening to the jury in an action for damages against the caterers, he was carried away by the humour of a wedding reception in chaos. His brilliant gifts of description and humour had the jury roaring with laughter at the predicaments of the bridal party and the wedding guests as everything went wrong. It was a brilliant comedian's performance. However, George was supposed to get the jury worked up over the plaintiff's distress, so that she would be compensated with heavy damages. Instead they were so amused that they felt very modest damages would suffice. This was not one of George Reid's successes.

Successful persuasion depends very much upon the right mood in the person to be persuaded. Humour can come at the wrong time.

Where does one find a good joke? The late Bob Hope had a large staff looking for jokes and wisecracks for the master's shows. Hollywood has an industry for recycling jokes. Thus the old riddle: 'Which film star has the most hairs on his chest?' was answered in the 1920s 'Rin-tin-tin', in the 1940s 'Pluto the Pup', in the 1950s 'Lassie', and today, no doubt, 'Inspector Rex'.

There are volumes of jokes, some of which were published not so long ago. Some of the jokes are quite funny; many are rather broad in their attitude to the sexual and eliminatory functions. In fact, many of these jokes might be best confined to 'smoke-rooms', restricted to males, if any still exist.

It is a problem as to how broad a joke may be.

Audiences vary. Some people will not protest and pretend to be amused by a very broad joke, but in fact they are annoyed, even disgusted. There are still some words that are shocking to many members of a modern audience. Accordingly, a speaker needs to take care lest the joke or the language repels the audience.

After the *Lady Chatterley's Lover* case in England, the Anglo-Saxon synonym for 'copulate' became a word which an author, a playwright or a film producer could get away with. The famous F word is now used ad nauseam and has served to pad out bad prose, bad poetry and bad speeches. The constant use of the word is a good indication that the speaker has little that is useful to say. *Lady Chatterley's Lover* was originally written partly in order to make the F word acceptable. Instead the book was banned until, some years after the war, in a famous court case, a prosecution of the publisher for publishing an obscene book failed. The case was hailed as a landmark for freedom of expression. Now I wonder whether the decision released a word into general usage which might have been better retained as an effective expletive.

These days, one needs to be careful lest attempted humour contravenes the modern rules of politically correct speech. It can even land a speaker before the criminal courts if there is a racial slur or attack contained in a speech. This is most likely to occur when an attempt is being made to be funny. Slurs on women are also likely to produce a well deserved hostile reaction. It is well to remember that some of the jokes of yesterday may be very counter-productive today. There is a long list of derogatory words frequently used yesterday, the use of which today is absolutely prohibited not merely by social convention but often by the law. A nervous speaker trying to be funny can often find that the speech has entered a forbidden area, and the results can be serious.

It is a fact that a great deal of humour rejoices over the misfortunes of others. It is safe to assume that even today in a stage show or film, someone slipping badly on a banana skin will receive laughter, not sympathy. Even the old custard tart in the face still gets a laugh, but it must not be racially directed, nor must it strike a disabled person or a young child, and so on.

The restrictions on the cruelties of yesterday are by no means a bad thing. Take as an example the old nineteenth-century 'humorous' poem by Thackeray, the ballad of 'little Billee', which contains the 'funny' lines:

> Oh Billy! We're going to kill and eat you,
> So undo the button of your chemise.

This is an example of how far the idea can be taken that the misfortune of others is funny. In the nineteenth and early twentieth centuries a lot of people found the idea of cannibalism funny. Thus there were innumerable cartoons of missionaries boiling in cooking pots. This style of humour is not considered nearly so funny today.

The poem by Thackeray was inspired by the wreck of the yacht *Mignonette*, where the crew of three – captain, mate and cabin boy – took to the life-boat. They were starving so the two men killed the cabin boy, ate part of his body and survived. After their rescue, they were quite open about what they had done, and as a result they were tried for murder in the leading case of the *Queen v Dudley and Steven*. They were convicted. Their defence of necessity was rejected as a legal exoneration, but after some time they were pardoned.

Even today, there is still an enormous amount of humour based upon human misfortune. But one should beware lest there be too much sympathy for the person in trouble, so that the joke falls flat and the audience may be repelled, or even disgusted. The danger of this can always be avoided by telling the story against oneself. Then if you think it is funny that may well be good enough for the audience. You are not laughing about another person's misfortune.

Humour can often be achieved by putting one concept into a completely different context, or comparing unlikes. Thus Mark Twain could write a very funny book about a 'Connecticut Yankee at the court of King Arthur'. Horses can be compared with humans as in *Gulliver's Travels* by Jonathan Swift.

Humour can be achieved in many ways. Some people are said to have no sense of humour, but this is usually quite untrue. Their idea of humour is simply different from yours. The skill is to find humour that will appeal to all or most of the audience.

One must always try to judge the audience. Humour may be out of place or it may not come off. Obviously in a speech commemorating a train crash or some tragedy, humour will be out of place. On the other hand, at wakes, and even during funeral eulogies, humour is quite common.

An after-dinner audience usually wants to be amused and will meet the speaker halfway. On the other hand, it can happen that an audience can be out of sorts, and almost impervious to good jokes.

If a good joke falls flat and it is not an old chestnut, it is probably because it was not told well. However, it may be that the fault was not that of the speaker but of the audience. If it appears that the audience is a difficult one, it may be best to forget trying to be funny and press on with a serious speech.

The manner of telling the joke, the words chosen, the facial expression and the tone of voice are, if anything, more important than the joke itself. Timing is especially important. Timing is one of the greatest assets of a comedian or, for that matter, a tragic actor. It is a great asset for any speaker.

Some speakers laugh with the audience, some merely smile and sometimes the speaker is deliberately either mournful or 'deadpan'. In these regards, if you copy a successful speaker you will almost certainly come to grief. Your style must suit yourself, not someone else.

In a persuasive speech, humour can serve as sugar for the message pill; it can be a vivid illustration; it can establish maximum audience contact. However, the speaker must bear in mind always that the main object is to persuade, not amuse. Humour should assist but not submerge the speech.

19.

Emotional appeal and exaggeration

THE DIFFERENCE BETWEEN REASON and emotion is vividly illustrated by the marriage of Benjamin Disraeli. At the age of thirty-five in 1839, he married a lady fifteen years older than himself, quite deliberately for her money. Parliamentarians were not paid in those days but lived expensive lives. 'I may commit many follies in life,' he said, 'but I never intend to marry for love.'

Mary Anne Disraeli, white-haired at the age of fifty when she married Benjamin Disraeli, made him a perfect wife. She was a rich widow, neither brilliant nor beautiful but she studied Disraeli for a year before she married him and their subsequent marriage was one of the love stories of the century. He often joked with her that he married her for her money but would do it again for love. Although he wielded political power much earlier when the Tories were in government, Disraeli did not actually achieve the eminence of prime minister until 1874. Sadly, by then, his darling Mary Anne was dead and could not share in his ultimate achievement.

Thus one may say that Disraeli's decision to marry Mary Anne was rational, if somewhat callous, but his love for her was purely emotional. But was it? She made him a perfect wife, despite being at times foolish and scatter-brained. She never lost faith in his ability to succeed, and there were many despondent moments in his political life when he needed her comfort. He, on the other hand, became her adoring husband. For thirty years, their marriage was near perfect.

This story illustrates that the line between the emotional and the rational is hard to define with any accuracy. It is, at best, a wavy line, but an important one.

As counsel for the accused in criminal trials, barristers were supposed to confine themselves to rational non-emotional arguments. No Sydney counsel could expose his female client's naked beauty and thereby secure an acquittal from an admiring assembly, as did the counsel of Phryne, the famous Greek courtesan, in ancient Athens.

Of course, counsel sailed as close to the wavy line as they could, and they no doubt still do. Thus one was not entitled to say of the young man who happened to kill another young man in a pub brawl that he had a wife and children who would be in great trouble if he went to gaol. That would be a purely emotional argument. But one would be entitled to call the wife and mother of his children to give evidence of his good (and gentle) character, and to attest that he was a good father. That evidence would lead to the rational arguments that he would be unlikely to commit a criminal offence, and that he was a person likely to tell the truth when sworn as a witness. So says the Law.

The famous firm of Howe and Hummel of New York in the roaring 1920s was alleged to have provided attractive wives and children for their clients. The bogus wives and children sat in the courtroom looking appealingly at the jury throughout the trial. That might be defined as using purely emotional tactics for the purpose of an argument.

According to Shakespeare, when Caesar was murdered, Brutus argued rationally and eloquently to the Roman crowd. However, Mark Antony prevailed by appealing to their emotions. Pointing to a gaping wound in Caesar's body he shouted: 'See what a rent the envious Casca made'. Shakespeare's play is often cited to support the proposition that the emotional argument or appeal will always prevail over the rational. I doubt this. Much depends on a multitude of circumstances, but there is no denying the power of an emotional appeal. Sometimes it is absolutely necessary in order to drive home a point.

Probably one of the greatest causes of misery in modern life is bullying. It occurs in schools, defence establishments, offices and factories. It is opposed by often-repeated platitudes, but little in the way of determined action. It is frequently the fact that the bully is popular, not only with his or her mates but also with the authorities, and often has powerful friends. On the other hand, the victim is almost invariably unpopular. 'He [or she] asked for it,' says the world. And so bullying goes on, unchecked despite the usual platitudes uttered by those who should eliminate it. (I spent six years in boarding school up to the age of twelve. I saw a lot of bullying, but I do not recall any bully ever being punished by the school authorities. Sometimes we did the punishing ourselves, but rarely, because bullies were usually popular and had plenty of support. I was lucky in that my father had me taught boxing when I was about ten years old.)

However, every now and then, but with almost monotonous regularity, a victim of bullying is badly hurt. Despite the best endeavours of the authorities to hush it up, the bad news leaks out to the media and there is a public outcry. One month it may be a schoolboy, the next a soldier, the next a factory apprentice. Wherever it occurs, there is a stern protocol against that sort of thing, a protocol that is strong in words, but rarely enforced.

When there is such a public victim, there is a short outcry, perhaps there is a scapegoat or two, and the whole wretched business continues again after a short interval, as though nothing had happened. How often have I read about initiation ceremonies, often brutal, and sometimes even indecent?

Do the authorities who knowingly or negligently permit bullying ever get punished themselves? The victims usually have to leave the relevant establishment and start again elsewhere.

Rational argument has done nothing to eliminate bullying and very little to reduce it. The authorities often say, 'We had to put up with it ourselves and it did us no harm. It toughened us up.' Most importantly, the authorities are far more concerned about protecting the reputation of the institution than admitting a problem and dealing with it.

In circumstances such as these, the emotional argument may get through whereas the rational argument hits the old answer: 'We agree; there is no real problem; this is a one-off situation and we are dealing with it. We already have a protocol against bullying.'

The emotional argument may be effective by stirring up strong feelings. An emotional description of an injured soldier or schoolboy can cut through the usual hypocrisy in these cases of bullying and force the authorities to do something real rather than feigned. An emotional account of the privileges in private schools and military colleges, the expensive facilities and the great opportunites, will make the public much less ready to overlook abuses. The public would be reminded that these institutions are richly endowed while hospitals lack elementary facilities and so on. More should be expected from the privileged. Noblesse oblige.

The emotional appeals would be to horror and disgust (at what happened to the victims) to anger at privilege abused, even to envy of those who cannot afford these privileges. Reference would be made to the lesser facilities and privileges of other people so that more might be expected from those offenders.

Such emotional appeals may well have a firm, logical foundation in rational argument, but the emotional appeal may succeed where rational argument has failed. Emotional argument has a force, a thrust and an impact that mere rational argument lacks. A person presenting an emotional argument will feel the emotion expressed, just as a good actor lives, rather than acts, the part. When Dickens read aloud to his audience the death of Nancy from *Oliver Twist*, he suffered all of Nancy's terrors and felt all of Bill Sykes' rage. As a nightly experience, it became a menace to his health. Dickens was not so much acting as living the parts he read, hence the strain on his health. He became mentally and physically exhausted and died of a stroke. Many modern actors live, rather than act, parts and acting can be a very strenuous profession.

An emotional argument is felt, sometimes very deeply indeed, by the speaker, and this feeling makes a powerful impact on the audience. The speakers who make this impact are sincere and they feel the emotion they are expressing. Many speakers let themselves be carried away by their own emotion. There are powerful films of Martin Luther King delivering his 'I have seen the promised land' speech. Although emotion can be feigned, deeply felt emotion transfers itself easily to the audience.

It is not necessary for emotion to be loud and obvious. If one compares the speeches of Adolf Hitler with those of Winston Churchill, one can see in the latter a restraint that is even more powerful than the shouted declamations in the former. The speeches of both of these men were among the most effective in history, for evil and good respectively. Each used emotion, but probably Churchill was more effective. Of course, each man was giving a different message to different audiences.

Beware of feigned or pretended emotion. It rings untrue and, in most cases, the speech seems pretentious and foolish. It is best to use emotion in a speech only when it is genuine. The idea then is to let it flow, let it inspire you, but do not let it control you. Many a speaker, in particular politicians, has later regretted loose and foolish language expressed in an emotional outburst. It is very easy to lose control of your reason when you loosen the reins on your emotions.

I have often said that in advocacy and public speaking you must never lose your temper. Whatever anger you may feel or express, you must retain control. The same applies to an emotional speech. It is hard not to let your feelings run away with you, but the consequences of letting this happen can be serious.

Considerable problems arise when emotions enter into speech-making. There is a strong tendency to exaggerate or twist facts to suit the flow of feeling. Emotional attachment to a cause is likely to blind one's eyes to the true facts.

The problem is accentuated by public attitudes. Just as there is poetical licence to twist the facts in the cause of art, so an audience may excuse the emotional speaker who is light on reason and facts. It is hoped that the audience not only makes allowances for the speaker but preserves mental reservations about the message in the speech.

As I pointed out in my chapter on the ethics of persuasion, appeals to the emotions are the weapons of those who pervert the art of persuasion. Appeals can be made to prejudice, hatred, and racial suspicions, just as in better causes they may be made to love, compassion and mercy.

The use of emotion is fairly simple. A rational outline of a speech is prepared, then it is enlivened and illustrated with emotional material from which comes the emotional appeal itself.

Let us imagine a speech aimed at securing greater expenditure on public hospitals. You prepare a rational outline to the effect that people are waiting months, even years, for surgery, that understaffing and overworking must lead to mistakes. Now you add the material about human suffering: the person who was deaf and waited over two years for an operation, several times attending only for the operation to be cancelled; golden staph crippling or killing patients in hospital for routine surgery; the mother with two young children who died in the waiting room before being attended. These examples are based on facts, but the speaker would be wise to quote chapter and verse, that is he should, if possible (subject to privacy considerations) give names, dates and places.

Then out come the stops. How terrible for a person to be deaf for years when a simple operation will cure it; how frightful that a routine patient should die or be crippled by infection in this, the twenty-first century; how can an alleged civilisation permit a young mother to die unnecessarily through the wanton neglect of politicians?

One can pull out further stops and become even more emotional. Where did the money go which might have saved the young mother's life: on parliamentary pensions; on fireworks at New Year's Eve; on Olympic games (let it go – be very emotional) to be won by drug-doped contestants, as more and more exposures seem to reveal?

One can now work up to the issue of whether the

politicians care. Do they wait in a public hospital queue or do they receive red-carpet treatment at a private hospital?

And so it can go on. One can ponder what was fair, what went too far in the above example. But, as in the case of bullying, an example I gave before, hospital reform has been the subject of a lot of words and not that much effective action. In fact, it may well be that public hospitals today are worse than yesterday. Might the emotional appeal get through when all else fails?

Note how the examples chosen are extreme instances. It is headline news if a young mother dies unattended in a hospital waiting room. It is hardly a daily occurrence, but as the speaker in my example works up steam, you will envisage dead bodies daily in every hospital waiting room, ignored by indifferent politicians.

It can be readily seen that the emotional appeal tends to fly off the rails of reality. In this case, it might have been more effective in restrained terms, but who knows? In arguing a case for better hospitals, you will obviously make more impact with dramatic examples than with dull statistics (which few thinking people will believe). In any event the Government always has its own statistics ready to hand.

Of course, one could make this appeal more effective still by finding an example of a neglected child. Happily our children's hospitals are too good to provide many examples of neglect of young patients.

To what extent are you entitled ethically to use emotional appeals in speeches? Surely one is entitled to appeal to pity, compassion, love of one's fellow citizens, but to what extent is it fair to appeal to the general dislike (even hatred) of bureaucrats and politicians?

According to political sources, apparently most citizens of New South Wales are terrified of crime and criminals, even if criminologists say the crime rate is declining. Our politicians apparently believe that this terror is a good source of votes and the political parties conduct an auction of severity for convicted criminals. Often barbaric mandatory sentences are advocated, particularly, but by no means always, for crimes of violence. I was amazed to hear the Premier of New South Wales boast about how many people were in gaol. Only one or two commentators noted that this large gaol population was not mainly comprised of violent criminals but of relatively, if not completely, harmless social misfits, illiterates and intellectually disabled persons who probably need help rather than punishment.

Whenever there is a victim of a notable newsworthy crime, he or she is asked was the court's punishment enough. Not unnaturally, it never is. It can be seen that these speeches on crime and punishment play on two of the strongest emotions, fear and revenge. Revenge, of course, is another form of hatred.

We cannot doubt how effective are speeches appealing

to fear, hatred and revenge. Not so long ago, such speeches caused the lynching of many black Americans in the southern states of the USA. I shall always remember the photo of a black man burning alive, while an audience, including a young child, watched. Appeals to fear, hatred and revenge led to Nazism and the Holocaust. There is, indeed, a danger in appeals to these emotions.

I advise speakers, as they acquire the power to reinforce logical arguments with appeals to the emotions, to beware. They have acquired a powerful weapon that can be a force for good or evil. A good speaker needs to perfect a complete code of ethics, and adhere to it, and never cross the line where an emotional speech becomes an evil speech.

It is well also to beware of the end supposedly justifying the means. It rarely does.

It is not for me to compose a code of ethics, because subject to the basic rules of truth and fairness, it is for the speaker in the particular circumstances to judge what is right or wrong. I simply draw attention to very real dangers. Perhaps it is well for me to repeat that being unfair, untruthful and misusing one's power to appeal to the emotions may well bring you loud applause. Do not be intoxicated by undeserved cheers.

Linked with emotional appeals is exaggeration. This can be an arresting way of illustrating a point. For example: if drunken drivers were gibbeted beside the highways, their bodies would certainly deter other drivers from driving when drunk. This is an impossible, ridiculous but arresting example to illustrate that severe punishment may well prevent crime. (However, when such ideas were actually tried in the eighteenth century they failed because so few criminals were caught.)

Many extravagant statements are not intended to be taken literally and are true hyperboles. As such, they do no harm and are useful to emphasise points, or serve as vivid illustrations. The extreme example is often used in legal argument to test the validity of a proposition.

One must distinguish hyperbole so defined from the extreme statements made by a person under stress, or a speaker carried away by emotion. A true hyperbole is readily understood as not intended to be taken literally. Exaggerations under stress may well be assumed to be true, and accordingly they are dangerous.

On the subject of emotional appeals, one can hardly overlook the old Hebrew prophets and later Christian teachers. As I have said before, religious preaching is an exception to my fundamental proposition that a persuader should not provoke the audience. Preaching is usually aimed at securing the repentance and conversion of the congregation. Modern preachers tend to woo their listeners and gently instruct them, but certainly not always. It is a tradition of religious believers that they are all sinners – miserable sinners, it is often said. As such sinners, they can hardly complain if their shortcomings are revealed to them in no uncertain terms.

An audience can sometimes be persuaded to change its mind by shock tactics. It is made to feel guilty, to feel ashamed, even fearful, and thus it is readily persuaded to comply with the speaker's demands.

This style of persuasion is very successful at times. As I have said often in this book, people are not naturally bad and nasty, even if they fall far short of perfection. It is possible to reach an audience in many ways. The particular method described of reminding an audience of its own faults first appeals to the consciences in the audience, whether in a speech for social reform, or a sermon to secure better conduct. These days the arousal of guilty consciences usually has to have a fairly sound rational basis, but it can be done, and is often done. Emotional appeals may be made to justice, to fairness, to fear.

To sum up, an emotional appeal is a very powerful weapon for a speaker. It is a weapon that must be handled with great care, lest it controls the speaker as well as the audience, lest it be used for evil rather than good. Only practice will teach a speaker to ensure that he or she uses an emotional appeal as a servant, not a master.

20.

How to promote a cause

THERE IS A LOT about us that needs change and reform by government, whether federal, state or local. Politicians are often prompted to effect changes and reforms by pressure from the community, started by some public minded person. In my lifetime there have been many good causes such as Aboriginal land rights, national parks, environmental protection, aid to the disabled, improved health care, particularly mental health, and so on. There have been little local causes, such as obtaining post boxes, telephone booths, stop signs and so on. There have been organised oppositions to over-development or destruction of heritage buildings. Advancing public causes is a skilful and at times difficult exercise. This is where the gentle art of persuasion may well come into its own.

One of the most successful public campaigns in recent years was the campaign to free Lindy Chamberlain from prison. It ultimately prevailed against very strong opposition by the Northern Territory government. There was a Royal Commission and Mr and Mrs Chamberlain were pardoned then had their convictions quashed. They finally received compensation for all that they had endured.

Immediately after the verdicts of guilty against the Chamberlains on 29 October 1982, many people were horrified at the outcome of the trial. Of course, many others cheered. It was a divisive issue to say the least.

Azaria Chamberlain disappeared from the family tent at Ayers Rock (now Uluru) on 17 August 1980. Her mother, Lindy, said that she had been taken by a dingo and Coroner Denis Barritt so found on 20 February 1981. Barritt's criticisms of police and others provoked further investigations that resulted in the trial and convictions of the Chamberlains, she of murder, he of being an accessory after the fact to that murder.

Murder, without a motive, by the mother of a baby nine and a half weeks old is, to say the least, unlikely, unless the mother is suffering from post-natal depression. Lindy Chamberlain clearly was not so suffering. She was an apparently loving mother, and all the witnesses at the site that night enthusiastically proclaimed her innocence. She was nevertheless convicted on forensic evidence.

It was not surprising that many people, including prominent lawyers such as Sir Reginald Sholl, late of the Victorian Supreme Court, felt that there had been a miscarriage of justice. After all of the appeals had failed, there were numerous letters and meetings seeking a further inquiry into the case.

It is interesting to note how the campaign commenced by letters to politicians, and then there were public meetings, often attended and supported by the witnesses at Ayers Rock on the night of 17 August 1980. The enthusiasm of these witnesses was remarkable, but perhaps not so remarkable when it is appreciated that they were proved to be right.

Mrs Chamberlain was fortunate in her solicitor Stuart Tipple. His efforts, and those of her counsel, John Philips QC and Andrew Kirkham, had been outstanding at the trial against tremendous odds. He never lost faith in Lindy Chamberlain over years of struggle. He served to coordinate the efforts of everyone and keep them on a reasonably unified course. In particular, he advised the various Chamberlain support groups not to support a conspiracy theory that said that a tame dingo named Ding had killed Azaria and this had been covered up by the chief ranger, his deputy and other good people at Ayers Rock. This absurd theory, without any substance, could have been a basis for undermining the whole protest campaign. It illustrates how often in such campaigns one's worst enemies are one's purported allies.

There were pro-Chamberlain groups formed all over Australia, including in Darwin, and these were given unity and guidance by a Chamberlain Innocence Committee of which the chairman was Sir Reginald Sholl and whose membership was of prominent persons, parliamentarians, a former judge, artists, medical people and lawyers.

Altogether, the Free Lindy Chamberlain campaign was a model for pursuing a cause. It may be noted that, unlike some greenie movements, it always kept within the law, even though its meetings were vigorous and its protests were loud. (Anyone involved in such a public campaign would find useful material in the book *Innocence Regained* (Federation Press, 1989) by Norman Young, which deals in detail with what developed into a very effective public campaign.)

A public campaign may be commenced by letters to those in authority, public meetings and letters to the media. The usual problem is how to attract media interest, a problem that was not so great in the Free Lindy campaign because Lindy Chamberlain was always of interest, always newsworthy.

Many people do not appreciate how to get the ball rolling. Local members of parliament will nearly always give some attention to letters and communications from their constituents as will local councillors. Newspaper columnists are always looking for something new. Sometimes a letter to a newspaper will gain attention. All of these ideas worked for Lindy Chamberlain.

Another idea that worked for her was the signed petition. This usually goes to a parliament, and the government may act on it. If there are many signatures, it is hard for bureaucrats and ministers to ignore a petition completely. Petitions for Lindy were, in fact, rejected but they kept her cause alive, and before the public.

Care needs to be taken with petitions. Enthusiastic supporters sometimes sign them many times and even get children to sign them. This gives opponents an opportunity to discredit the petition.

The promotion of a public cause involves all sorts of persuasion, written letters, public meetings and personal canvassing of individuals to join or assist the cause.

In such a campaign, most of the suggestions I have made as to methods of persuasion apply. One seeks to persuade, not antagonise those in authority. Although many of Lindy Chamberlain's supporters wished to attack the Northern Territory government, and some did, those in charge of the movement realised that only persuasion would achieve their purpose.

As I have stressed, good persuasion is founded upon an accurate search for the true facts, and there were many investigations made by Lindy's supporters. The fresh findings were then conveyed to the Northern Territory government.

In the 1960s and early 1970s, there were quite a number of causes that were the subject of public agitation: conscription and the Vietnam War, and Aboriginal rights, political and land rights.

The Vietnam War protests were pursued very much on a party political basis, and with great bitterness. As a result, it is very difficult, even today, to find any sensible and reasonable discussion of the rights and wrongs of Australia's part in that war. These protests were very much concerned with confrontation rather than persuasion, and, after all, one may wonder what they really achieved. Certainly they vividly illustrate how political heat and confrontation can eliminate reasonable discussion and debate. It would be interesting, even now, to examine the history of this period to ascertain whether the noisy and bitter demonstrations and processions actually produced any changes of mind. I rather think that each party took up an entrenched position, so that reasonable discussion became impossible.

There was a completely different course taken in the many pro-Aborigine demonstrations from the early 1960s right up to the present time. It may be that these were accompanied by rational persuasion. It may be that once the problems were revealed, there were few who really wanted to deny political or even land rights to the Aborigines. No political party stood in the way of these rights. In fact, it was the conservative Liberal Party through Bill Wentworth that promoted the successful referendum of 1967. The student radicals who conducted the freedom ride in 1965 hardly met the opposition that occurred to such demonstrations in the USA, although in some towns they were not popular.

The Aboriginal demonstrations indicate that there is a real power in processions and demonstrations if they are conducted in a persuasive rather than a confrontational manner. There were many issues, but they were such that the public really only needed to be told of the problems. Once the problems are revealed, and information starts to flow in such cases, the cause is just about won. By and large, the Aboriginal problems of politics and land rights have been handled by those advancing the Aboriginal cause quite sensibly. It is just as well, since the problems now revealed of Aboriginal health, education and opportunity are very difficult to solve.

There have been other cases where convictions have been challenged (apart from that of the Chamberlains). It is interesting to note that the strange case of Alexander McLeod-Lindsay was reopened for the second time in 1991. There was a murderous attack by someone on his wife on 14 September 1964 and he was convicted of attempted murder on 5 March 1965. No motive was ever proved, or even suggested, in any evidence. It was this lack of motive as much as anything else that produced some public disquiet. There were reasonable submissions made to the New South Wales government and as a result there was an inquiry into the conviction. To the disappointment of his supporters, on 2 October 1969 this inquiry reported in favour of the conviction standing. However, fresh expert forensic evidence cast further doubt on the original conviction so a second inquiry was held, even after Lindsay finished serving his sentence on 3 August 1973 and his parole expired in 1982. In July 1991, the second inquiry found that there were substantial doubts as to Lindsay's guilt and he was subsequently pardoned and later compensated.

It should be noted that both the Lindsay inquiries were brought about by careful persuasive argument. No one was blamed, no one was accused. Least of all did anyone attempt either to confront or to blame the New South Wales government. Yet, being familiar with both cases, it would appear to me that the reasons for reopening the Lindsay case were never as compelling as those for re-opening the Chamberlain case. However, in the latter case, the Northern Territory government felt itself to be on the defensive. The case became politicised. It is not all that clear how that occurred.

Lindy Chamberlain was a non-Territorian, supported and represented by non-Territorians, and the first coronial findings had been very critical of Northern Territory officers and witnesses. The further investigation and the subsequent convictions of the Chamberlains became a triumphant response to that criticism. Hence the unedifying cheers that accompanied the verdict of guilty.

Thus it was that the Free Lindy movement came up against a rather unfriendly government. The case had become politicised, by and large through no fault of Lindy's supporters, still less of the Free Lindy movement.

It frequently happened in Europe and America that cases became politicised so that politicians' careers depended upon obtaining a conviction. It happened in England in the rather horrible Profumo affair. The Chamberlain case never sank to those depths, but at the same time carries a warning that politics and criminal justice should be kept well apart.

There are obvious dangers of confrontation, whether it be of governments, bureaucrats, police or one's fellow citizens. When the wild colonial boy, Jack Doolan, confronted the troopers, the answer was a volley of rifle-fire which killed him. Confrontation normally produces a hostile reaction.

This is by no means to say that there should never be confrontation. Often there simply has to be. As the Second World War showed, persuasion in the nature of appeasement is sometimes regarded as weakness, and confrontation then becomes the only reasonable course of action. Every barrister who has practised in the criminal law is well familiar with confrontation, and the need for confrontation. However, wise counsel will usually regard confrontation as a means of last resort.

Persuasion should not provoke adverse reaction, even if it fails. Confrontation makes enemies; bitter confrontation makes bitter enemies. This may be necessary, but one should not rush into danger.

When promoting a cause, as enthusiasm rides high, restraint is essential if unnecessary opposition is to be avoided. For example, if a landholder is concerned lest his property be affected by an Aboriginal land claim, his worst fears will be confirmed and his implacable opposition will be ensured if he is described as a racial bigot. This is a case where, if progress is to be made, his misgivings should be carefully heard and understood. Then it may well be that his opposition will cease.

The great difficulty about public causes is that they give some people a chance to go all out and let off steam. Politicians are abused, derided and insulted, even physically assaulted. Opposition speakers are shouted down. The sad fact is that quite a few people enjoy trouble, even violence, and if they are your supporters, their efforts may well lose your cause.

Hatred of the opposition appeals to many. It may even create a fellowship of haters. Australia was never more united than during the war when we all hated Germans and Japanese. In war this is inevitable, but it should not occur in peacetime in disputes between citizens.

One act of hatred leads to another, and this has been especially so in many Green agitations for environmental causes. Confrontations, breaking the law and dangerous stunts usually only operate to swing public opinion against the cause advocated, and to strengthen the opposition. The crowd that booed Menzies won him votes. Many an industrial strike has been lost because of senseless violence, whether to persons or property.

In the promotion of a cause, stupid excesses and unnecessary confrontations on the part of your supporters may well defeat the cause. These excesses and confrontations need not be as extreme as to produce violence, but even stupid statements, the result of excessive zeal, can be used with deadly effect against a cause. It is not unknown for wild statements, even violence, to be deliberately provoked by those pursuing a cause, as a means of discrediting the opposition.

During the Second World War, Arthur Calwell, then Minister for Information, took wartime censorship way past preventing the disclosure of information to the enemy. He censored adverse political material criticising the government. The law was that censored material could not result in a blank in a newspaper. Each blank had to be filled in so that no hint of censorship appeared. The newspapers then agreed together to publish the blanks and some of the censored material. Calwell then purported to ban the newspapers and Commonwealth police were sent to stop the newspapers going out on the streets. It was a difficult task for them.

At the premises of Ezra Norton's *Daily Mirror*, an enthusiastic staff refused to obey the Commonwealth policeman, so he stood in front of the delivery truck to prevent it leaving. The staff then pelted the unfortunate officer with bales of newspapers. In a panic, he drew his gun and pointed it at the driver who was then revving up the engine. Of course, a photographer then quickly took a photo of a quite desperate policeman with his drawn revolver menacing the truck driver. Provocation had succeeded. The next edition of the *Daily Mirror*, which came out very quickly, showed Calwell's 'Gestapo' menacing the freedom of the press. The public was enraged.

Calwell backed down in the High Court, as much for political reasons as for legal reasons. It is an old tactic, provoke your opposition into doing something, or saying something, really stupid, and you have created great propaganda for your cause. A lot of semi-violent protests aim at producing stupid acts on the part of the police particularly, but modern policing should, and usually does, include training to meet such situations.

When I was acting for the Department of Education, a troublemaking teacher sought to address a school.

The headmaster banned him, and the media gathered. Fortunately I was in time to advise the department to let the troublemaker in, and in he came. But the demo fell very flat. He was hoping to be arrested for trespass. I doubt whether many bothered to listen to his speech after he got in.

Similarly, when a notorious agitator was working off a few fines in the Women's Prison, she ostentatiously kept a diary of her prison life, and, as she hoped, the officers tried to take the diary from her when she was released. Fortunately, they later followed my advice and let her keep the diary. There was no story for the media waiting outside and I never heard of the diary again. The main idea of the diary had been to provoke a newsworthy confrontation.

A mild answer turneth away wrath but nothing annoys an agitator more than compliance with his or her demands.

The point I wish to make is that if you have a good cause to promote with rational arguments, beware of stunts and provocation. Sometimes they get publicity, but it is bad publicity. Usually they not merely make the cause unpopular, but they embed and solidify the opposition of those whose compliance is sought.

Promoting a cause is an essential and useful part of the democratic system. If you are prepared to do so reasonably and rationally, on most occasions you will succeed. The authorities actually do want to do the right thing. If they fail to do so, they will as often as not bow to media pressure and public protest, so long as they are not provoked into implacable opposition.

21.
Written submissions

IN THE MAIN, THIS book has dealt with oral persuasion, but most of the ideas expressed apply to written submissions as well.

I have discussed the need for repeating and emphasising the message in a speech; otherwise the point may be lost, although emphasis and repetition may sometimes be necessary. However, the reader can re-read passages not understood on the first reading. A dictionary may be employed if necessary, if the author of the paper chooses to display an extensive vocabulary. There is not the same concern as in oral persuasions that the message will not be comprehended.

But was the written submission read at all? Often you

never know. When written submissions became mandatory in the New South Wales Court of Appeal, we all took some pains in writing them, envisaging learned judges of appeal poring carefully over what we wrote. For myself, I was somewhat surprised to find quite often that my cherished work had not even been read. I was comforted by the amusement raised for me by judges pretending they had read my submissions when they obviously had not, and who were now rapidly scanning them so as to be able to claim some knowledge of what I had written. Later judges did read written submissions as a matter of course, and I assume that they still do.

Of course, when they read them, there was almost invariably a complaint, either that they were too long or too short. It was interesting to ponder beforehand which it would be, even to venture a guess. Gradually a pattern developed as to what was expected, and the complaints were fewer, or at least about some other aspect of the submissions.

So, the first consideration in drafting written submissions is to estimate how long the paper ought to be.

Unfortunately, in many learned papers these days it is believed that the longer the paper the more learning it contains, a belief that is usually quite wrong. Far too many papers, and court judgments for that matter, spend many weary pages displaying the erudition of the author before coming to the point. When the point is ultimately reached, it is often obscure rather than clear.

It is not as though many people read the many pages of learned discussion with copious footnotes. Most executives these days scan impatiently through to the conclusion, hoping, often in vain, to find the point.

I see no reason why it is necessary to 'pad' written papers with material that is rarely read and serves little purpose. A written submission should not be padded. This may well occur in an ex tempore speech, even a good one, but in a written submission the padding cannot be mercifully forgotten as in a speech. It is there every time the paper is read. A good written submission should be similar to a good speech. The message should be clear and it should be quickly introduced so that the reasons for the message are quickly apparent. It should conclude in such a way as to summarise and emphasise the message. In the case of a persuasive submission, it should be quickly made clear what is sought to be persuaded, and the arguments in favour should follow. Thus the reader will know the reason for the arguments. Then the message of persuasion should be summarised and emphasised at the conclusion.

All of these are fairly basic rules. One can depart from them and succeed, but it is risky to do so.

It is surprising how many word and grammar errors are made in a speech. A transcript of an apparently good speech can reveal many slips and errors. It is expected that a written submission will be carefully checked, and that there will be few errors.

The speaker can watch the audience and form some idea of its reaction. If the wrong note is struck in a written submission, the author gets no chance to correct it.

In Edward Fitzgerald's translation of *The Rubaiyat of Omar Khayyam* occurs the fifty-first verse:

The Moving Finger writes; and, having writ,
Moves on: nor all thy Piety nor Wit
Shall lure it back to cancel half a Line,
Nor all thy Tears wash out a Word of it.

I once quoted this to a solicitor who wanted me to rearrange an opinion I had written so as to hide part of it.

It is an important thought. What is said in haste may well not be heard, and is often quickly forgotten. Writing has a permanence that can be very inconvenient.

'That is not what you said last week' can be the subject of dispute. What you wrote is there to be read. The careless words of an enthusiastic orator may perhaps be forgiven, if not forgotten, but the deliberate words carefully written down cannot be easily excused.

The author may not appreciate the likely mood or feelings of the reader, and give unnecessary offence quite unwittingly. If written submissions contain defamatory matter or insults, this is at the risk of the author, and it is a serious risk. Care is obviously desirable for everything you say, but for what you may write it is essential.

In particular, it is dangerous to let off steam against someone in writing. You may feel differently when the writing is actually read, but that is, to say the least, difficult to explain to the reader.

A written submission to pursue some cause should not be dashed off in haste. It should be written carefully and read again by the author, not just to check for errors but to re-check the substance.

These days with computers it is easy to dash off a few thoughts then fiddle about, and re-adjust until a very rough draft becomes a neat, carefully drafted document. The many drafts may well reflect changed thoughts and attitudes as the subject receives closer consideration. In my opinion, these drafts should be destroyed. They can only give a false impression since your considered submission occurs only in the final version.

There may be some point in conserving drafts of negotiations between different parties. Only confusion and misconception can result from saving drafts of one's own thoughts, before making up your mind.

Although when I was in a practice I often used the computer method of a very rough draft altered and re-altered till I was satisfied, I am inclined to think that better results are obtained by thinking the document through in your mind and then dictating or writing, as nearly as possible, a final version. In the old days of type-writers, where the typescript could only be altered with difficulty, and not very neatly, people had to learn to get it right the first time. This is now rather a forgotten art.

Writing differs very much from a speech in that it can, and should, be checked before it is completed. One can read a written speech, but a speech directly made to an audience cannot be checked. When checking the substance of a written submission, you should try to read it as others will understand it, and see whether that matches your original intention. If not, it can be corrected or amended.

The written submission gives the reader time to think and consider. The idea is to so draft it that the more it is considered, the more convincing it will be.

In my experience, I found that cases and disputes were settled more easily and frequently if there was a face-to-face discussion, rather than by correspondence. The telephone would often serve in place of a face-to-face discussion but was not as effective. It was more impersonal and one could not judge reactions as well.

It is arguable as to which is more effective, but I believe that the oral submission is better than the written submission in the art of persuasion because one can usually appreciate the reaction of the listener and adapt the submission accordingly.

Conclusion

IN THIS BOOK, I often refer to the unpleasant sides of human nature, but I hope I have shown that in all of us there is good and bad. I believe that the good is stronger in the average person. Hence I hope that if this book assists to persuade people to advance causes, the persuasions and causes will be for the benefit, rather than the detriment, of my fellow citizens.

If you manage to acquire an ability to persuade, you hold it in trust for your community to use it for good. I hope I have assisted you.